FUTURE BEAUTY

FUTURE BEAUTY

FUTURE BEAUTY
30 YEARS OF JAPANESE FASHION

Akiko Fukai, Barbara Vinken, Susannah Frankel, Hirofumi Kurino
Edited by Catherine Ince and Rie Nii

First published 2010 by Merrell Publishers Limited
in association with Barbican Art Gallery on the occasion
of the exhibition *Future Beauty: 30 Years of Japanese Fashion*,
October 15, 2010 – February 6, 2011
Haus der Kunst, Munich, March 4–June 18, 2011

Published by Merrell Publishers, London and New York

Merrell Publishers Limited
70 Cowcross Street,
London EC1M 6EJ

merrellpublishers.com

Barbican Art Gallery
Barbican Centre
Silk Street, London EC2Y 8DS

barbican

barbican.org.uk

This edition published 2013 by Merrell Publishers on the occasion
of the exhibition *Future Beauty: 30 Years of Japanese Fashion*,
Seattle Art Museum, June 27–September 8, 2013
Peabody Essex Museum, November 16, 2013 – January 26, 2014

Seattle Art Museum
1300 First Avenue
Seattle, Washington 98101

seattleartmuseum.org

Peabody Essex Museum
East India Square
Salem, Massachusetts 01970

pem.org

Exhibition co-organized by Barbican Art Gallery and the Kyoto Costume Institute
Curated by Akiko Fukai, Director/Chief Curator of the Kyoto Costume Institute,
and Kate Bush, Head of Art Galleries, Barbican Centre.
The exhibition was generously supported by Wacoal Corp.

The Seattle Art Museum (SAM) exhibition was organized by the Kyoto Costume
Institute in collaboration with SAM. The Peabody Essex Museum (PEM) exhibition
in Salem, Massachusetts, was organized by the Kyoto Costume Institute in
collaboration with PEM. The exhibition's presentation at PEM was supported in
part by the East India Marine Associates.

Additional support for the exhibition and the book
accompanying the exhibition was provided by SHISEIDO CO., LTD.

Additional support for the book accompanying the
exhibition was provided by the Asahi Shimbun Foundation

Edited by Catherine Ince, Curator, Barbican Art Gallery,
and Rie Nii, Associate Curator, Kyoto Costume Institute
Chronology compiled by the Kyoto Costume Institute,
with additional research by Flavia Loscialpo and Kendall Martin
Assistant Curators: Ariella Yedgar, Corinna Gardner
Exhibition Assistants: Jessica Rolland, Juliette Desorgues
Interns: Sophie Sheldrake, Kendall Martin

British Library Cataloguing-in-Publication Data.
A catalogue record for this book is available from
the British Library.
ISBN 978-1-8589-4546-0

Produced by Merrell Publishers Limited
Designed by John Morgan studio
Copy-edited by Philippa Baker
Indexed by Vicki Robinson

Printed and bound in China

Front cover: Cindy Sherman, *Untitled*, 1994,
costume designed by Rei Kawakubo/Comme
des Garçons; see page 24
Page 3: *Rei Kawakubo/Comme des Garçons*
Autumn/Winter 1983–84, photograph
by Naoya Hatakeyama; see pages 74–75

FOREWORD
SEATTLE ART MUSEUM

The inspiration and transforming innovation of contemporary Japanese design is brought to life with *Future Beauty: 30 Years of Japanese Fashion,* curated by the esteemed fashion historian and director of the Kyoto Costume Institute, Akiko Fukai. Launched on the world stage in the 1980s, the groundbreaking collections of the designers featured in this exhibition have had a profound impact on the global world of couture ever since.

The Seattle Art Museum (SAM) is honored to present *Future Beauty: 30 Years of Japanese Fashion,* our first exhibition of fashion design. Northwest audiences will be especially enthusiastic and perceptive viewers because of their enduring personal, institutional and regional connections with Asia and Asian art. Our renowned collection of Asian art is the foundation on which the museum originated, and it remains an integral part of our mission and identity. Exquisite examples of textiles and kimonos from different historical periods in our Japanese collection and our strong contemporary art program provide a deep and rich context for the exuberant and pioneering visions presented in *Future Beauty.*

Western couture for women has traditionally centered on accentuating the body with symmetry of the silhouette as a defining characteristic, but Japanese designers in the 1980s boldly questioned these assumptions and presented radical alternatives. They deconstructed many of the basic premises of Western design and reformatted the relationship between body and garment. Designers Issey Miyake and Kenzo Takado were already well established in Paris fashion circles in the 1970s, and in the early 1980s Rei Kawakubo and Yohji Yamamoto introduced a stark new aesthetic based on monochrome black and white, asymmetry, and organically flowing designs that rippled across the fashion world.

Future Beauty focuses on the different thematic elements of these Japanese designers' interest in the structural relationship between a garment's flat, folded form and its three-dimensional embodiment, a relationship that inspired fearless creativity and extraordinary fashion. In collaboration with Japan's renowned textile manufacturers, designers created structured synthetic fabrics that have a volume and memory independent of the body, producing startling sculptural effects while retaining a beautifully crafted economy of design.

In the decades since the 1980s, many designers have come to display their ingenuity by revisiting the history of couture and freely playing with a stock of Western and Japanese references that can be deconstructed and reinvented. In recent years, the influence of a youth-oriented Japanese street style has been the catalyst for diverse and entirely different kinds of fashion trends, which can be appreciated for their ingenuity and recognized for their impact on high fashion—yet another provocative dimension to this fascinating exhibition.

Future Beauty's thematic presentations vividly illustrate the richness and diversity of different generations of designers. In addition, Curator Akiko Fukai has chosen to showcase works by such revered design pioneers as Issey Miyake, Rei Kawakubo—founder of Comme des Garçons—and Yohji Yamamoto, as well as two younger and extraordinary innovators, Junya Watanabe and Jun Takahashi, to highlight their significant contributions. The exhibition not only provides inspiration for fashion insiders, artists, and designers, but also is a memorable visual experience that will capture the imagination of our visitors.

First and foremost I would like to thank Akiko Fukai, for her curatorial vision and the great expertise she brings to this project. Deeply knowledgeable about the postwar international fashion developments, she understands the groundbreaking ideas of the Japanese designers in a much broader context. The exhibition draws from the contemporary side of the Kyoto Costume Institute's extensive collection of more than 11,000 exquisite pieces, which date from the eighteenth century to the present day. I would particularly like to pay tribute to Wacoal Corp. and its representative director, president and CEO, Yoshikata Tsukamoto, for the enlightened vision that led to the creation of the Kyoto Costume Institute in 1978—a gift to world culture. A number of individual pieces come to us directly from the designers, and we would like to extend our great appreciation and warmest thanks to Issey Miyake and Yohji Yamamoto for their support.

At the Kyoto Costume Institute, our special thanks go to Curator Rie Nii for her attention to every detail during the planning and implementation process. We gratefully acknowledge the assistance of Tamami Suoh, Makoto Ishizeki, Naoko Tsutsui, Kumiko Tomonari, and Hiroshi Ashida. Akiko Fukai originally developed this exhibition in collaboration with Barbican Art Gallery Director Kate Bush and Curator Catherine Ince in London in 2010, where it was enthusiastically received. SAM's Susan Brotman Deputy Director for Art and Curator of European Painting and Sculpture, Chiyo Ishikawa, was greatly inspired by *Future Beauty* at the Barbican and was instrumental in bringing this outstanding exhibition to SAM.

Our colleagues at the Barbican Art Gallery in London have been extremely generous in sharing their insights, materials, and equipment, and we are grateful for their support. We are delighted that *Future Beauty* will travel from SAM to the Peabody Essex Museum (PEM) in Salem, Massachusetts. For their thoughtful contributions during the planning of the exhibition, well-earned credit goes to PEM Director and CEO, Dan L. Monroe; Priscilla Danforth, Director of Exhibition Planning; and Lynda Roscoe Hartigan, the James B. and Mary Lou Hawkes Chief Curator.

Finally, as a project of this scope is never created without the participation of many people, I would like to extend a special thank-you to our Museum team and their staffs for the successful realization of this exhibition at SAM: Catharina Manchanda, Jon and Mary Shirley Curator of Modern and Contemporary Art; Vice Director Maryann Jordan; Chris Manojlovic, Exhibitions Designer; Lauren Mellon, Interim Director of Museum Services; Nicholas Dorman, Chief Conservator; Zora Hutlova Foy, Senior Manager for Exhibitions and Publications; and Sandra Jackson-Dumont, Kayla Skinner Deputy Director of Education and Public Programs.

We are confident that audiences in Seattle, a city known for its trailblazing spirit and fearless innovation, will find tremendous inspiration in this breathtaking exhibition.

Kimerly Rorschach
Illsley Ball Nordstrom Director
Seattle Art Museum

FOREWORD
PEABODY ESSEX MUSEUM

*The vernacular of beauty ... remains a potent instrument
of change in this civilization.*

Dave Hickey, *The Invisible Dragon: Four Essays on
Beauty* (1993)

For a Eurocentric audience, the word "beauty" evokes timeless
ideals, values, and truths as well as a universal culture of taste.
Yet in 1993, when art critic Dave Hickey published his
influential book *The Invisible Dragon: Four Essays on Beauty*,
he knew full well how controversial the concept of beauty had
been for our culture and for many contemporary artists since
the 1960s. Its association with the superficial, the commercial,
and the constrained had disqualified beauty as an agent for
change and a bearer of meaning. Hickey argued the contrary,
calling out the fluid, complex, and often contradictory nature
of beauty as the very source of its relevance for testing the
shifts in art and culture that we experience.

Although Hickey's frame of reference was contemporary
Western civilization, his observations remind us that different
times and different people have their own perceptions of
beauty. Historically, in the West we have objectified beauty
according to standards of perfection. Simultaneously we
have also regarded beauty as elusive and undefinable, to be
experienced subjectively through mind, emotion, and spirit.
This dichotomy has not existed in Japanese interpretations,
which consider beauty to be an internal, intuitive state of
being that is an integral part of daily life. The Japanese so
value transience and imperfection as expressions of beauty
that these qualities have fostered an abiding appreciation
of asymmetry, roughness, simplicity, austerity, subtlety,
and aging in all things natural and man-made.

Transience and imperfection suggest change and
freedom from convention, and it is this point that looms
large in assessing the worldwide impact of Japanese couture
since the early 1980s. Such designers as Issey Miyake,
Rei Kawakubo, and Yohji Yamamoto led the way in
redefining the relationship between clothes and the body,
overturning Western conventions of fashion in the process.
This publication persuasively articulates the intent and
design vocabulary that accomplished this, yet one point
merits emphasis: the future of beauty, as negotiated by
recent Japanese designers, has flowed from their profound
understanding of the subtle symbiosis between tradition
and innovation.

The Peabody Essex Museum (PEM) is tremendously
pleased to be one of two American venues for *Future
Beauty: 30 Years of Japanese Fashion*. PEM is dedicated to
transforming people's lives through deeper, personalized
engagement with global art and culture as well as the many
facets of creativity; in concert these provide a compelling
means of understanding our place in the world. This
aspiration informs our exhibition program, which values
the unexpected as a catalyst for exploration. The changes
that Japanese fashion has effected have indeed been
unexpected, and not simply because of a different approach
to form, construction, materials, and palette. Even more
transformational is the contribution that Japanese fashion
has made to recalibrating the relationship between "East"
and "West" as sites of culture and creativity. Japanese
designers have proposed something different: interpreting
their culture's perception of beauty, not as an exotic "other"
for the West, but as an avant-garde for a global community.

This acclaimed exhibition marks a critical chapter for PEM's new initiative, which in 2009 introduced contemporary fashion as an interpretive complement to one of the country's leading collections of historic costumes and textiles from around the world, including Japan. Garments that reflect an individual's place or role in society have generally been deemed traditional, while apparel that reveals prevailing customs of a period, country, class, or occupation is usually considered costume. These definitions align with the definitions of material culture rather than fashion, which is an of-the-moment realm of beautiful, personal style. But reasons for which we wear something, and the way in which we do so are inextricably bound to creativity as an interpreter of identity. "To fashion," after all, is to make something with imagination and ingenuity, using shape and form to mold or transform.

PEM is also home to one of America's oldest and largest public collections of Japanese art, originating with the museum's inception in 1799, some fifty years before Commodore Matthew Perry ended Japan's self-imposed exile. Holding some of the earliest works brought from Japan to America, our collection includes many works that cannot be found in Japan today and features a breadth of objects that deal with Japanese art and culture, especially of the eighteenth and nineteenth centuries. It is a great pleasure to share with our audience an exhibition that so eloquently expresses Japan's contemporary creativity.

We owe immense gratitude to the Kyoto Costume Institute, especially Director/Chief Curator Akiko Fukai and Curator Rie Nii, for organizing this compelling exhibition and for collaborating so fruitfully with us. We warmly thank the Seattle Art Museum (SAM) and its director Kimerly Rorschach for partnering with us to bring the exhibition to this country, and recognize the contributions of Zora Hutlova Foy, Senior Manager for Exhibitions and Publications, and Catharina Manchanda, Curator of Modern and Contemporary Art. PEM staff has once again brought its considerable talents and teamwork to bear, and we particularly thank Priscilla Danforth, Director of Exhibition Planning; Juliette Fritsch, Chief of Education and Interpretation; Dave Seibert, Director of Exhibition Design; Kathy Fredrickson, Director of Exhibition Research and Publishing; Claudine Scoville, Head Registrar; and their staffs. The Museum's East India Marine Associates has graciously provided support for our presentation.

Finally, we salute the artists featured in *Future Beauty: 30 Years of Japanese Fashion* for their daring. In their designs we have ample evidence of the depth and richness of beauty as one of the most provocative concepts in human history.

Dan L. Monroe
The Rose-Marie and Eijk van Otterloo Director and CEO

Lynda Roscoe Hartigan
The James B. and Mary Lou Hawkes Chief Curator

Peabody Essex Museum, Salem, Massachusetts

FUTURE BEAUTY
30 YEARS OF JAPANESE FASHION

Akiko Fukai

Japanese Fashion Today

Today, the phrase 'Japanese fashion' evokes a strong image. Japanese fashion is probably best known to people around the world in the form of the low-cost, high-quality ethic of such labels as Uniqlo, 'Tokyo street style' or *kawaii*. Originally meaning 'a tender feeling for something young or child-like or small', or, more succinctly, 'cute', *kawaii* is now used worldwide to refer to the cool contemporary culture of Japan. Both Tokyo street style and *kawaii* are characterized by popular appeal, youthfulness or even childishness, simplicity and occasionally vulgarity, exaggeration, artificiality and ornament – qualities related to such Japanese cultural forms as manga, anime and video games.[1] However, Japanese fashion covers far more than the colourless adjective 'Japanese' would suggest, as a brief look at its history reveals.

In the 1960s, with the burgeoning of mass youth culture, fashion in the West became a social phenomenon and the ready-made clothing industry grew considerably. Riding on the coat-tails of this growth, Japanese fashion also made a great leap forward. Kenzo Takada's debut in Paris in 1970 added considerable momentum to this advance, and over the decade such designers as Issey Miyake and Hanae Mori became well known. Since then, with the expansion of the Japanese economy, ever-increasing attention has come to be focused on the country's fashion.

Although Paris remained the centre of the fashion world around 1980, such developments as the rise of punk in London and the growing ascendency of Milan – on the shoulders of which the hopes of Italian fashion rested – made it clear that couture everywhere was undergoing a period of vibrant energy. Backed by economic prosperity at home, an increasing number of Japanese designers began showing their work in Paris, London and elsewhere. Rei Kawakubo of Comme des Garçons and Yohji Yamamoto debuted in Paris in 1981, and immediately Japanese fashion, often termed 'avant-garde', garnered worldwide attention.

This proved more than just a temporary phenomenon. While Kawakubo and Yamamoto are still active today, a younger generation of designers – including Junya Watanabe, who made his Paris debut in 1992; Jun Takahashi of Undercover, who debuted in Paris in 2002; and Dai Fujiwara, currently in charge of Issey Miyake – followed in their footsteps. Now, the latest generation of designers is emerging as the new pillars of Japanese fashion. These designers have carved out a niche for themselves that has undermined the hegemony of Western fashion and exerted a major influence on the course of world couture. Their work, and the images and discourse that have been constructed around it, is set apart by the meaning and function of the aesthetic they express.

Couture Clash

In October 1982 the word 'Japanese' featured prominently in the headlines of newspaper articles reporting on the Spring/Summer 1983 fashion collections. Ten of the seventy or so shows held in Paris over that season were by Japanese designers.[2] While the sheer power of these numbers was widely noted, what divided the critics was the shock of the garments unveiled by Kawakubo and Yamamoto.[3] Throughout 1982 trade disputes had been breaking out between Japan and France, mainly over automobiles and electrical appliances, and the French newspapers gave prominent coverage to these disputes while remaining wary of the inroads being made by Japanese designers.

Paris was already well acquainted with Japanese designers. Kenzo was seen as a designer who typified Parisian fashion, and Miyake was also highly regarded.[4] In 1977 Mori had become the first Asian woman to be made a member of the exclusive Chambre syndicale de la haute couture in Paris, a branch of the governing body of the French fashion industry, the Fédération française de la couture, du prêt-à-porter des couturiers et des créateurs de mode; and in April 1981 Kenzo, Miyake and Kansai Yamamoto had featured in an article in the *International Herald Tribune* under the headline 'Three Japanese Designers Make Big Dent in Paris'.[5] But although Rei Kawakubo and Yohji Yamamoto had both established themselves in Japan throughout the previous decade, they made their Parisian debuts of 1981 quietly. They were not yet members of the influential Fédération, and their Autumn/Winter 1981–82 and Spring/Summer 1982 collections were seen by only a handful of people. This included representatives of the French newspaper *Libération*, however, whose article was one of the first to feature these designers and accurately reported their work's important characteristics, including its emphasis on material, form and deconstruction.[6]

By March 1982 Kawakubo and Yamamoto had joined the Fédération, and they presented their Autumn/Winter 1982–83 collections in catwalk shows, as they have done ever since. Kawakubo presented a black sweater pierced with holes (which later became widely known through the photography of Peter Lindbergh), an ecru-coloured sweater given a daring sense of volume by its twisted stitches, and a white dress with drawstrings. All were perfectly proportioned. There was already a touch of the ragpicker in the way Yamamoto's models, who occasionally wore white masks, appeared to be almost dragging the oversized, tattered garments down the runway, although there were interesting details around the hemline to catch the eye.

The clothes proposed by Kawakubo and Yamamoto in October 1982 (Spring/Summer 1983 collections) were so shocking that critics responded with discomfort. The reporter for *Le Figaro* wrote that their collections sent a chill up her spine. She said of Kawakubo: 'Her apocalyptic clothing is pierced with holes, tattered and torn, almost like clothing worn by nuclear holocaust survivors'. The work of Yohji Yamamoto (who was mistakenly named as Kansai Yamamoto) was described as 'clothes for the end of the world that look as if they have been bombed to shreds'.[7]

There were also positive appraisals, however. In many areas of the press, the clothes of Kawakubo and Yamamoto were now recognized as representing something completely new. *Libération* and the *Washington Post* concluded that Kawakubo and Yamamoto were pioneering a new aesthetic.[8] The *New York Times* wrote: 'The fashions that have swept in from the East represent a totally different attitude toward how clothes should look from that long established here.'[9] These clothes may have stood outside the norms of traditional European aesthetics, but nobody could ignore their powerful originality.

What the Japanese designers of the 1970s had presented was not the 'East' as once expressed through the eyes of such Western designers as Paul Poiret, but clothing that blended Eastern and Western cultures, as seen through the eyes of the East yet still comprehensible to the West. In contrast, although they were thoroughly aware of European culture, Kawakubo and Yamamoto presented clothing that dared to impress on audiences an aesthetic that was far removed from this context. Robbed of a scale or point of reference by which to evaluate the results, audiences seemed disorientated. This was the genesis of what would become Japan's shake-up of the fashion world.

As well as attracting a good deal of media attention, with major newspapers in Europe and the United States devoting considerable space to them, Kawakubo and Yamamoto created shows that were henceforth unmissable for retail buyers. In the way the shows were put together, in the models' manner and style of walking and, in particular, in Comme des Garçons' style of make-up, which made the pale female models look scarred and haggard, the buyers sensed a freshness that was quite different from anything that had come before.

In March 1983 (Autumn/Winter 1983–84 collections) *Le Figaro*, under the headline 'Les Japonais jouent "Les Misérables"', was still dismissing Kawakubo's and Yamamoto's clothes as 'not fit to be worn by readers of *Le Figaro*'.[10] However, the Japanese designers were increasingly seen as a match for their French counterparts, as suggested in October 1983 by the *Herald Tribune* headline 'The Japanese and Paris: Couture Clash, Head-On; Eastern Contingent Setting Pace for the Spring-Summer Collections'.[11] European and American press accounts of Japanese fashion exhibited an attitude based on a naïve view of Japan as an exotic, far-off land, which the Palestinian–American literary theorist Edward Saïd termed 'Orientalism'. This was perhaps motivated by a wariness of the newly rampant Japanese economy. But Western commentators would eventually recognize the strength and freshness of Kawakubo's and Yamamoto's clothes – qualities that could not be diluted by the Eurocentric gaze. From around 1983, more opportunities arose for exposure in Western magazines, and Japanese fashion gradually secured its position in Europe and the United States as the embodiment of all that was avant-garde, innovative and new.

Buyers were quick to react, particularly in the United States, where even those collections produced by Yamamoto prior to his 1981 debut in Paris were sold. In May 1982, Kawakubo's clothes retailed in just one shop in Paris, but by March 1983 they were also available in Parisian department stores, and by the mid-1980s her tattered black garments could be seen in fashionable boutiques throughout Europe and the United States, laid out flat on inorganic grey shelves.[12]

The grammar of Japanese fashion became an important social phenomenon that characterized the 1980s and was subsequently inherited by a number of Belgian designers, including Martin Margiela, to become part of the everyday language of fashion in the twenty-first century. But what was this grammar, and why was the aesthetic of Japanese fashion regarded as so shocking?

A New Aesthetic Horizon

Today, ragged, loose-fitting, ripped, frayed black clothes pierced with holes are a common sight. In explanations of this style to the many people who reacted negatively when they first saw it, such Western precedents as the slashed clothes in vogue during the Renaissance and the punk approach of Vivienne Westwood were cited. But the holes, intentional flaws and cloth dangling in shreds in the clothes of Rei Kawakubo and Yohji Yamamoto represented a form of ornamentation with a frame of reference that came from outside Europe. The impression they created, which seemed to endorse shabbiness, eschewed the beauty traditionally sought in European clothes, and it was no surprise that they were seen as shaking the very foundations of European fashion.

Viewed in the context of Japanese culture, however, this form of expression is less mysterious. The tea ceremony established by Sen no Rikyū in the sixteenth century is but one manifestation of the unique Japanese principles of *wabi* – without decoration or visible luxury – and *sabi* – old and atmospheric – generating an aesthetic of warping and distortion.[13] Edo merchant culture, for example, endorsed the extreme opposite of extravagance and magnificent splendour in the form of a shabby refinement.[14]

Kawakubo and Yamamoto also dispensed with multiple bright colours, instead sticking to stoic achromatic palettes reminiscent of the subtle colour tones of *sumi-e* (monochrome ink-and-wash painting), as well as the writings of Juni'chirō Tanizaki. In his short book *In Praise of Shadows* (1933), Tanizaki located the essence of Japanese aesthetics in the harmony of shadows: 'We find beauty not in the thing itself, but in the patterns of shadows, the light and the darkness, that one thing against another creates,' he wrote.[15] The black clothing of Kawakubo and Yamamoto, the light and the darkness woven by thread, the shades of colour created when material sags and overlaps, skilfully incorporates shadows as a form of sartorial expression. As Kawakubo hinted when she stated that 'Red is Black', Japanese designers in general are able to distinguish various nuances in black, which integrates all colours.[16] In contrast to the elegance of the pure black used by such designers as Christian Dior and Coco Chanel, Kawakubo and Yamamoto played with the ambiguity of black, just as the existentialists in mid-twentieth-century Paris and the punks in London in the 1970s and 1980s used black – the colour of poverty and mourning – as an expression of social protest. At the same time, black, which Yamamoto described as 'an intellectual, contemporary colour', found a following among many other designers in the affluent 1980s as the colour of asceticism.[17] Eventually, towards the end of the 1990s, this ambiguity saw black taken up as a major trend, not only dominating fashion but also becoming the colour of the age.

Scene from *The Loss of Small Detail*,
Ballet Frankfurt, 1991
Choreography by William Forsythe
Costumes designed by Issey Miyake

Scene from *Scenario*, Merce Cunningham
Dance Company, 1997
Choreography by Merce Cunningham
Costumes designed by Rei Kawakubo/
Comme des Garçons
Photograph by Timothy Greenfield-Sanders

Ma

Making clothes is all about how to relate flat fabric to a three-dimensional figure in the form of the human body. European-style couture involves giving three-dimensional form to fabric by using curved lines and darts to fit it to the body. But Japanese designers were free from European couture methods, because of the notion of the kimono in their minds. The kimono, in contrast to the construction of Western clothing, is an assemblage of rectangular pieces of fabric; as a result, when not worn, a kimono is flat. It would be very natural, therefore, for Japanese designers to seek to create a new relationship between clothes and the body. Examples of this approach to the construction of clothing include simply draping a piece of flat fabric over the body, as in Issey Miyake's 'A Piece of Cloth' concept in 1976, and Rei Kawakubo's earlier works, which comprise two-dimensional sections that become inexplicably complex when laid out on a surface (as seen clearly in the photographs taken by Naoya Hatakeyama; see pages 67–77). In addition, the technique of origami often appears in Miyake's garments, and in those of Junya Watanabe, Koji Tatsuno and other Japanese designers.

It cannot be denied that such 'flat' clothes completely hide the curves and beauty of the female form. When a woman puts on one of these garments her shape is disguised in a way similar to the effect of a kimono, which simplifies her figure into a willowy column. Seen through European eyes, these items of clothing that allow maximum freedom within their accommodating shapes are perceived as loose-fitting and shapeless. Yet to the Japanese, the superfluous 'space' between the garment and the body, referred to as *ma*, is more than simply a void: it is a rich space that possesses incalculable energy.

In addition, such construction techniques are often accompanied by asymmetry, which the French literary critic and sociologist Roger Caillois described as a distinguishing characteristic of Japanese aesthetics.[18] Asymmetry can be seen most clearly in the clothing of Yohji Yamamoto. After creating deconstructed clothes in the 1980s, Yamamoto brought into play his knowledge of European couture to create his own distinctive tailored style, making exuberant use of couture techniques. From the mid-1980s, he gave clear expression in his clothes to an important current within twentieth-century fashion that revolved around bodily functionality, and since 2001 he has worked with Adidas to develop the Y-3 Sportswear line. Throughout this evolution, asymmetry has continued to be a distinguishing feature of his designs.

What the clothes of these Japanese designers have in common is that only when they are worn do they take their final form, and movement causes them to acquire further unexpected shapes. Rei Kawakubo's clothes from the 1980s were characterized by inexplicably intricate sections. When worn, the garments hang off the wearer with sections swaying in complex combinations. Kawakubo's garments represent an abstract three-dimensional form, a hidden three-dimensionality – only on the wearer's body does the garment evolve into a three-dimensional form. Becoming aware of the subtle interplay between the two-dimensional and the three-dimensional, and responding to the passion put into the clothes by the designer, the wearer is enticed by their intellectual playfulness. These characteristics are clearly revealed in a comparison of the flat garments with photographs of them restored to three-dimensional form. Yamamoto often says that his clothes are made half by him and half by the wearer.

That being the case, it is perhaps unsurprising that these characteristics should be most clearly expressed in dance costumes. The American dancers and choreographers William Forsythe and Merce Cunningham have both collaborated with Japanese designers: in 1991 Forsythe's Ballet Frankfurt performed in stage costumes created by Issey Miyake, while Cunningham was inspired by Rei Kawakubo's Spring/Summer 1997 collection 'Body Meets Dress, Dress Meets Body' (often referred to as the 'Lumps and Bumps' collection) to create the fascinating work *Scenario* (see opposite).[19] It is here that one can detect the *ma* of Japanese designers, or, to put it another way, the answer to fresh questions concerning the relationship between clothes and the human body.

Textiles and the Tactile

Another characteristic shared by many Japanese designers is their ability to create textures unlike anything found in existing clothing fabrics. By using these new materials in daring ways, they are able to create entirely new forms. They begin designing at the thread or textile stage, and are deeply involved in practically every process, up to the completion of each garment. This approach, clearly discernible in the work of designers from Issey Miyake, Rei Kawakubo and Yohji Yamamoto to those belonging to the younger generation, such as Akira Minagawa of Minä Perhonen, and Hiroyuki Horihata and Makiko Sekiguchi of Matohu, could be described as a traditional Japanese one in which the materials and the final form are inseparable. It is bound up with a modest attitude, summed up by Yamamoto when he states, 'In the final analysis, nothing is actually being created. Faced with fabric that is obviously going to be more beautiful the less one plays around with it, we designers are like swimmers wallowing in a tsunami or raging torrents.'[20]

From his debut in the 1970s, Miyake began creating clothes by making the fabric. Although he drew on his extensive studies of traditional Japanese dyeing and weaving techniques to create clothes with an extremely contemporary appearance, he also relied on the developmental capabilities of Japanese synthetic-fibre manufacturers. In the second half of the 1980s, these 'new synthetic' fabrics made from polyester were attracting worldwide attention. Since 1993 these and other advanced textile-development technologies have been incorporated into Miyake's groundbreaking 'Pleats Please' line. It could be said that, beyond the basic construction method of clothing with fabric and thread, this development in fibre technology and production process represented a step forward for the apparel industry, not least when the 'Pleats Please' line was followed by the 'A-POC' collection, unveiled in 1999 and an extension of the 'A Piece of Cloth' concept of 1976. In 'A-POC', Miyake, with Dai Fujiwara, was to develop a weaving process that produced fully finished garments without the need for sewing. Material, form and function are independent of one another yet at the same time strongly interrelated, hinting at a new couture process. To the extent that he opened doors not just in clothing design but even more so in clothing manufacturing, Miyake is truly looking into the future.

The Japanese designers who attracted so much attention with the holes and tears in their fabric also have an interesting perspective on materials. In the late 1970s Vivienne Westwood adopted the practice of making tears and holes in her garments as an expression of protest directed at the Establishment. This had the effect of breaking down the image cherished by the fashion industry, which demanded that skin, which is imperfect and fragile, should be completely hidden or daubed with all manner of gorgeous products. Kawakubo and Yamamoto adopted the same technique as an expression of protest directed at European hegemony.

In the late twentieth century, the equation of clothing as skin – fabric covering the body – played a part in reassuring the uncertain self. Fashion also showed a renewed interest in tactility, and a new awareness of the skin was embodied in the vogue for piercing and tattooing. One can argue that, in the sense that clothes are a second skin, the ripping of garments suggests the act of tearing human flesh. For the cover of a pamphlet in 1988, Yamamoto chose a photograph by the British photographer Nick Knight of a rough surface resembling a close-up of the flesh of an animal with a pattern of lines that look like incisions (see opposite). In this context Kawakubo's and Yamamoto's act of making tears and holes in clothes (where fabric is a metaphor for the skin) could be described as an act aimed at helping the wearer to find a new self.[21]

Japanese fashion thus sought to deconstruct European aesthetics and to encourage people to reconsider their Western ideals of beauty. The expressions of Yamamoto and Kawakubo, originally described as 'avant-garde' and 'shocking', came in the 1990s to be called 'grunge' – a term that has now spread all over the world. At last fashion, which had seemed hesitant to step into the postmodern realm, moved to a new level and began to explore fresh possibilities in garment design.

Fashion as Media

Fashion is involved in a cut-throat battle with the passage of time. From the moment it enters the world, it is already a thing of the past. Images, including photographs, play an enormous role in drawing attention to the existence of fashion, for which the present is everything, and in linking it to the future. Japanese fashion, which has featured in the pages of countless Western magazines since the 1980s, has been strengthened in this way. There is no question that the distribution of these images by various means, including publicity photographs, catalogues and pamphlets, although traditional, remains an important strategy in contemporary fashion.

In 1978 Issey Miyake published the book *Issey Miyake: East Meets West*, widely disseminating his own style and demonstrating a clear understanding of the importance of print media. Since then, he has continued to publish one groundbreaking book after another, often featuring the work of renowned American photographer Irving Penn. In addition, Yohji Yamamoto has worked with such photographers as Nick Knight, David Sims, Ferdinando Scianna, and Inez van Lamsweerde and Vinoodh Matadin (see opposite, top) to produce photographs that have fixed his clothes in the minds of viewers.

From the very beginning of her career, Rei Kawakubo has paid close attention to the special qualities of print media as she strives to give expression to her image of fashion. After she began showing in Paris she published a book of photographs titled *Comme des Garçons* (1986) featuring work by, among others, Hans Feurer and Peter Lindbergh, whose images have since been reproduced extensively in books and magazines. Also legendary is her biannual magazine *Six*, published from 1988 to 1991. Before this, from 1975 to 1981, Kawakubo had issued her own monthly PR magazine consisting solely of black-and-white photographs featuring her clothes. The folio-sized pages of *Six*, however, were filled with mysterious shapes that called to mind tactile sensations, and with recurring curves and rectangles, over which were collaged photographs of Native American female figures or nostalgic landscape photographs. Elsewhere there were photographs of works by Gilbert & George and Enzo Cucchi, and portraits of John Malkovich, Issey Miyake and Jean Paul Gaultier. This overlapping of dramatic images of works by artists and photographers from various genres was presented in a bold layout, confusing the reader but at the same time arousing the senses, stimulating what Kawakubo obliquely referred to in the title of her publication as the sixth sense.

These publications are an indication of Kawakubo's ambition to 'try expressing myself outside fashion'. 'By no means does the expression of the things I imagine reach completion through fashion alone', she has commented.[22] Kawakubo also continues to produce a direct mail in order to send a strong message to people everywhere. What comes through particularly clearly in her use of print media is a new perspective on femininity. As a symbol of strength both intellectual and graceful, Kawakubo's new female figure has transcended the conventional *femme objet*. With her direct mail for Comme des Garçons in 1994 featuring photographs by Cindy Sherman (see pages 23, 24), she dealt a clear blow to the cliché of 'woman as object' as seen in fashion photography at the time. Initially, the Western media often described the clothes of Kawakubo and Yamamoto as nun-like – a result of the designers' determination to go beyond the narrow framework of clothes created to make women appear beautiful.

Rather than appealing directly to consumers through pure advertising, Japanese designers have sought to create images or other vehicles that convey their own creative concepts. Miyake, for example, was one of the first Japanese designers to adopt the exhibition as an expressive medium, beginning with *Issey Miyake: Bodyworks* in 1983, followed by *Energies*, presented at the Stedelijk Museum, Amsterdam, in 1990 (see opposite, bottom), and, more recently, the dramatic installation *Making Things*, first shown at the Fondation Cartier pour l'art contemporain, Paris, in 1998.[23] In 1989 Yamamoto collaborated with Wim Wenders on the documentary *Aufzeichnungen zu Kleidern und Städten* (*Notebook on Cities and Clothes*), which was commissioned by the Centre Pompidou and shed light on Yamamoto's clothes, his role as a designer, his approach to his work, and Tokyo as a work environment.

Japanese designers interpreted contemporary fashion intellectually, viewing it as but one in a range of fruitful expressive media available to them. This approach found expression in their active intervention in the creation and dissemination of images outside the fashion conventions of their time. In the 1980s and beyond, when the boundaries between fashion, design and art were being severely shaken, this attitude created the opportunity for Japanese fashion to attract the attention of art critics, curators and other art professionals.

Cindy Sherman
Untitled, 1994
Costumes designed by Rei Kawakubo/
Comme des Garçons

Recycling Tradition

There is no doubt that the labelling of Japanese fashion as avant-garde in the early 1980s was a response to the creative and original spirit of those Japanese designers who were striving to go beyond existing and conventional fashion concepts. In 1986 the exhibition *Japon des Avant Gardes 1910–1970* (*Japanese Avant-Garde 1910–1970*) at the Centre Pompidou in Paris exposed a cultural side of Japan – at a time when the country was attracting attention around the world for its economic growth – that also defined this Japanese spirit as avant-garde. The exhibition focused on aesthetics and concepts that existed beyond the realm of European thought; in other words, it focused on ideas that could not be discussed in any European language. Of course, the Japanese avant-garde being referred to here was avant-garde in a Western sense, but much of what appeared 'avant-garde' already existed in the Japanese tradition, such as the concepts of *wabi*, *sabi* and *ma*. These aesthetics and concepts existed outside a modern Western society, but clearly appealed to those in the West who were trying to escape from dominant Western cultural ideals or grappling with the inadequacies of the modern era. This cultural questioning was not irrelevant to the labelling of Japanese fashion as avant-garde. Its aesthetics were, in many respects, identical to what would later come to be labelled 'deconstruction' in the postmodern West.

These examples of Japanese fashion indicate how Japanese traditions are discontinuously continuing. The current moment might be viewed as a transitional time, in which a chaotic world is groping for a new social framework for the twenty-first century through style and design. Amid the trend towards increasing uniformity in fashion around the world, original techniques that are peculiar to specific cultures and distinctive aesthetics that have been handed down within these cultures are particularly relevant. As a part of this process, the past is linked to the present and to the future. Issey Miyake's clothes, given concrete form through new methodologies, still correspond with traditional ideas. In Rei Kawakubo's approach of reducing everything to zero and attempting to create in a completely new way, glimpses of the underlying aesthetics of Japan's past appear. And, although Yohji Yamamoto occasionally looks back at the past without distinguishing between East and West, the style behind his inherently European clothes is the quintessentially Japanese aesthetic of *iki* – sophisticated and possessing erotic charm.

From the late nineteenth century the Japanese, fascinated by Western fashion, pushed their own clothing culture aside and followed the styles of so-called 'international' fashion wholeheartedly. However, from the 1970s, a period when European clothing traditions were recognized unquestioningly as universal, Japanese designers started to transform the modern international language of fashion. They took certain elements – black, a tattered style, flatness, an interest in process, an intellectual approach and expression stemming from different contexts – and shaped them into a bold expression that opened European eyes to the existence of non-European aesthetics. This came as a shock to the West. Japanese fashion revealed the benefits of ceasing to perceive Japan as an exotic marginal culture and demonstrated that clothes born from non-European spheres can have universality. This was more than just a temporary shock. These Japanese designers led the charge into the postmodern realm and the twenty-first century.

Cindy Sherman
Untitled, 1994
Costume designed by Rei Kawakubo/
Comme des Garçons

1. 'Tokyo street style' is the unique fashion worn by young crowds in Tokyo's Shibuya and Harajuku districts since the mid-1990s. The peculiarly Japanese aesthetic of *kawaii* was articulated as early as the eleventh century by the author of *The Pillow Book*, Sei Shōnagon, when she wrote: 'All small things are adorable.' Manga are comics and printed cartoons in Japanese language, often presented in black and white and as serialized stories. Anime (abbreviation of 'animation') refers, in English, to a Japanese style of picture animation.

2. Rei Kawakubo (Comme des Garçons), Kenzo, Hiroko Koshino, Junko Koshino, Issey Miyake, Hanae Mori, Junko Shimada, Yuki Torii, Kansai Yamamoto and Yohji Yamamoto.

3. Representative of the critics was Nina Hyde, 'Japan's Runway Look', *Washington Post*, 16 October 1982: 'Shows by more than 50 designers will be held in the next five days; but the Japanese already may have conquered the Paris fashion scene.' In an article titled 'L'Offensive japonaise' (The Japanese Offensive) in *Le Figaro*, 15 October 1982, Martine Henno wrote: 'In 1983, is there a "yellow peril" on the horizon?' (editor's translation). She viewed the rise of the Japanese icily, but contended that, from a business standpoint, one could not help but accept it. Another article, 'Sept Japonais ethniques' (Seven Ethnic Japanese), *Libération*, 19 October 1982, stated that in terms of fashion, the Japanese had been recognized in Paris.

4. Henno 1982: 'The first was Kenzo. It was in April 1970. Today, twelve years later, he has become the best face of French fashion' (editor's translation).

5. Hebe Dorsey, 'Three Japanese Designers Make Big Dent in Paris', *International Herald Tribune*, 7 April 1981.

6. Claire Mises, 'Prêt-à-Porter 1982', *Libération*, 17–18 October 1981: 'They find their inspiration in the same source: it feels like the Middle Ages as seen in a film by Mizogushi [sic]. Perhaps there is more rigour in Comme des Garçons' work, giving a completely atemporal quality to [the] clothes. They look as if they have been worn for some time ... Ohji [sic] Yamamoto nearly achieves the same refinement, in a more obvious way ... These two stylists emphasize the unstructured aspect of the clothes, the suppleness of the fabrics' (editor's translation).

7. Janie Samet, 'Printemps/Été 1983, 6 Jours de Mode' (Spring/Summer 1983, 6 Days of Fashion), *Le Figaro*, 21 October 1982 (editor's translation).

8. Michel Cressole, 'Sept Japonais ethniques', *Libération*, 19 October 1982: 'Last March, following the global shake-up that had shattered the verities of the fashion and cultural worlds, the girls from Comme des Garçons (namely Rei Kawakubo) went into exile' (editor's translation). Nina Hyde, 'Japan's Runway Look', *Washington Post*, 16 October 1982: 'Yamamoto and Kawakubo are showing the way to a whole new way of beauty.'

9. Bernadine Morris, 'From Japan, New Faces, New Shapes', *New York Times*, 14 November 1982. Morris continued: 'They aim to conceal, not reveal, the body. They do not try to seduce through color or texture. They cannot be described in conventional terms because their shape is fluid, just as their proportions are overscale. Where the hemline is placed or where the waistline is marked is immaterial.'

10. Janie Samet, 'Les Japonais jouent "Les Misérables"', (The Japanese play 'Les Misérables') *Le Figaro*, 18 March 1983: 'The shocking Japanese were rude (30 minutes late) and had issued the seventh row for the representatives of *Le Figaro*, "non grata" VIPs. Because our readers are not supposed to become their clients. Correct! This miserablism is not for you. Neither are these patched-up clothes, nor these brand new rags, nor these fabrics tied up hastily like tatters. Nor all this funereal black. Nor the livid make-up of drawn-looking women. Snobbery in rags that bodes ill for things to come' (editor's translation).

11. Hebe Dorsey, 'The Japanese and Paris: Couture Clash, Head-On; Eastern Contingent Setting Pace for the Spring-Summer Collections', *International Herald Tribune*, 14 October 1983.

12. Mariejo de Loisne, 'A l'Est, du Nouveau' (News from the East), *Gap*, May 1982, p. 118, wrote that sales of Kawakubo's clothes in Japan were robust. They were sold in the United States at Henri Bendel, Bloomingdales and Macy's San Francisco, among other stores. In Paris they were sold at Victoire only, but by March 1983 they were available at Galeries Lafayette. The American fashion-industry journal *WWD* wrote in its issue of 16 March 1983: 'Paris – The contingent of Japanese designers who have become part of the fashion establishment here have relinquished neither their favored colors, black and white, nor their unconventional shapes for Fall. Tied, knotted, jagged and layered, the clothes retain the stark impact for which they have been celebrated in recent seasons. And this season they have maintained their high level of innovation and creativity in textiles.' When the Autumn/Winter 1982–83 collections were shown in Spring 1982, the names of Kawakubo and Yamamoto began to appear in the buyers' popularity polls of the French fashion industry *Journal du Textile*, and in March 1983 they made a rapid ascent, with Yamamoto ranking eleventh and Kawakubo twelfth (Kenzo was third and Issey Miyake seventh).

13. Sen no Rikyū (1522–1591), the Japanese tea master who perfected 'the way of tea', is known for *wabi*-tea (or *soan*-tea), 'humble tea' that created a sense of tension by reducing excess to the bare minimum. One could say that Mies van der Rohe's concept of 'less is more' is related.

14. Ihara Saikaku (1642–1693), one of Edo Japan's foremost literary figures, depicted the fashionable men and women of the early Edo period in his novels, describing in acute detail clothing that was often the antithesis of gorgeous extravagance.

15. Juni'chirō Tanizaki, *In Praise of Shadows* [1933], trans. Thomas J. Harper and Edward G. Seidensticker, Rutland, Vt. (Tuttle Publishing) 1977, p. 30.

16. Rei Kawakubo, 'Red is Black', theme for Autumn/Winter 1988–89.

17. Yohji Yamamoto interviewed by Akiko Fukai in *WOWOW* television programme, Tokyo, 19 November 2002.

18. Roger Caillois, *La Dissymétrie*, Paris (Gallimard) 1973.

19. Ballet Frankfurt, *The Loss of Small Detail*, choreography by William Forsythe and costume design by Issey Miyake, first performed 1991. Merce Cunningham Dance Company, *Scenario*, choreography by Merce Cunningham, music by Takehisa Kosugi, and stage and costume design by Rei Kawakubo, first performed 1997.

20. Yohji Yamamoto, press pamphlet, Spring/Summer 1993. The pamphlet continues: 'It's fabric. Beautiful as it is, we want to handle it, push it. It's like a current, it draws us in. But I didn't make anything, really. Not this time.'

21. See Akiko Fukai, 'Hifu to Hifuku (Skin and Clothing)', in *The Faces of Skin*, book on International Symposium, Tokyo, The National Museum of Western Art, 2001, pp. 48–55.

22. Yoshiko Ikoma, 'Interview with Rei Kawakubo: Jiyu to hankotsu seishin ga watashi no enerugigen na no desu (Freedom and a defiant spirit are my energy sources)', *Bijutsu Techo* (December 2009), pp. 107–108.

23. *Issey Miyake: Bodyworks* exhibition, 1983: Laforet Museum Ikura (Tokyo), Otis Parsons Gallery (Los Angeles), San Francisco Museum of Modern Art; 1985: Boilerhouse, Victoria and Albert Museum (London). For a chronology of Issey Miyake's exhibitions, see Makoto Ishizeki, 'Centralizing the Marginal: Japanese Fashion through the History of Fashion Exhibition', *Dresstudy*, vols. 57–58 (2010).

THE EMPIRE DESIGNS BACK

Barbara Vinken

To speak of 'Japanese fashion' is paradoxical. If it were national, it would not be fashion but traditional costume. Nobody would speak of Jil Sander, Helmut Lang or Martin Margiela as creating German, Austrian or Belgian fashion respectively. Similarly, Coco Chanel made not French fashion, but simply fashion. There are fashionable cities – Parisian chic, Milanese elegance, the New York look, London punk and Tokyo trash have become almost proverbial – but not fashionable nations. Fashion exists only at the moment at which it spreads and is worn – at least by a certain class or peer group – across the globe.[1]

Designers from Japan first came to international attention in the middle of the twentieth century through the work of Kenzo Takada, famous for his fantasy folklore in gaudy pop colours, and Hanae Mori, who, although more oriental than the most oriental-inspired Parisian designers, aimed to surpass and perfect European fashion (see overleaf for both). The second generation of designers from Tokyo – Issey Miyake, Rei Kawakubo (Comme des Garçons) and Yohji Yamamoto, known as the Big Three – fundamentally revolutionized our – Western – concept of fashion.[2] Following the first Comme des Garçons show in Paris, in 1981, fashion was never the same again. The revolution brought about by this second generation from Japan was not, however, the result of their work simply being foreign, other or authentic – that is, Japanese. Had this been the case, the clothes would have belonged in an ethnological museum rather than on the runway. Rather, it was because these designers deconstructed the West's centuries-old notions of the beautiful and the erotic. The history of Western fashion is the fabric from which their clothes were made. Their dialogue with the West was sometimes full of gentle humour, sometimes characterized by biting wit. What they showed *ex negativo* on the catwalk were our own Western ideas of fashion, masculinity, femininity, elegance and eroticism. Displayed and displaced, our concepts were exposed.

The triumph of the trio from Tokyo on the international stage – their reference to the Western idea of fashion coupled with their simultaneous success at turning it upside down – can be described, to paraphrase Salman Rushdie, as 'the empire designs back'.[3] Their clothes never fulfilled or surpassed what we understand as fashion, as did those of Mori and Kenzo in the generation before: rather, they disfigured and reconfigured our notion of fashion. They 'designed back'.

Rei Kawakubo is the most systematic and radical of the three in her deconstruction of the Western idea of fashion. Ever since her European debut in 1981, she has aroused scandal with beautiful regularity – a talent she has passed on to her protégé Junya Watanabe. The most recent highlight of this art of provocation was the Spring/Summer collection of 1997, 'Body Meets Dress, Dress Meets Body', which was immediately nicknamed the 'Lumps and Bumps' collection (see page 31). It transformed the model – so the bad-mouthing went – into Victor Hugo's Hunchback of Notre-Dame.

The deconstructive potential of this collection is immediately obvious. In Western fashion, fabric is cut and pinned to size on the body. A perfect dress fits like a glove. Through sophisticated tailoring, the body is idealized and sublimated. The simplest form of this idealization is symmetry, which is regarded as the norm of beauty. Lacing or padding may form part of this idealization, which serves to standardize and eroticize the body. The 'broad-shoulders, narrow-hips' erotic ideal for a man is given a helping hand by shoulder pads, while the hourglass figure of a woman is indebted to similar artificial enhancements: push-up bras and corsets or bodices that conceal the stomach or emphasize the hips. In the eighteenth century, hip pads called *paniers* made skirts so wide that it was almost impossible to pass through a door; the nineteenth-century *tournure* or *cul de Paris* made the bottom stand out invitingly. In the twentieth century, such tricks were no longer put on display as man-made but were instead naturalized, made 'real to the feel', as the lingerie store Frederick's of Hollywood would advertise. But throughout history, whatever body part was emphasized and whether this emphasis was made to look real or artificial, the body remained strictly symmetrical.

Kenzo Takada/Kenzo
Autumn/Winter 1981–82
Photograph by Niall McInerney

Hanae Mori
Autumn/Winter 1993–94

CRINOLINE in its NAKED MONSTROSITY shows that great difficulties have to be overcome in order to disguise the human form.

CRINOLINE with spasmodic efforts endeavours to enter a CAB. The low, vile, impudent Cabman laughs at the attempt. (Very remarkable!)

Crinoline, its difficulties and dangers:
a series of twenty illustrations from nature
Published in *Quiz*, 1850

Top: *Yohji Yamamoto*
Autumn/Winter 1986–87
Womenswear catalogue cover
Photograph by Nick Knight

Bottom, left: *Rei Kawakubo/*
Comme des Garçons
Spring/Summer 1997
Photograph by Niall McInerney

Bottom, right: *Vivienne Westwood*
Autumn/Winter 1995–96
Photograph by Niall McInerney

Japanese designers have produced many variations on the elaborately constructed undergarments that support a skirt. Following the principle of modern architecture that bares rather than conceals its technical construction, for her Autumn/Winter 1995–96 collection Rei Kawakubo designed a dress that uncovered the supporting *tournure* (see page 172). For his Spring/Summer 2003 collection, Junya Watanabe for Comme des Garçons laid bare the construction of the Rococo silhouette by showing the *grands paniers* of the gala toilette, *à la* Marie Antoinette (traditionally worn, of course, underneath the dress), as the dress itself (see page 203). And for Autumn/Winter 1998–99 he similarly transformed the crinoline from an undergarment into a dress (see page 204). Yohji Yamamoto, in his breathtakingly elegant Spring/Summer collection of 1999, used inflatable rubber tubes to fabricate a crinoline that could be worn without the skirt; function turns ornamental. A constant influence in Yamamoto's fashion shows is the *robe à l'anglaise* – a kind of manteau robe worn in the late eighteenth century, the upper part closely following the body while the skirt bagged luxuriously. This is just the effect highlighted by Yamamoto for Autumn/Winter 1986–87 in one of his best modern interpretations of the garment: a dazzling red *cul de Paris* bursts triumphantly out from the austere, simple dress, as seen in a famous series of photographs taken by Nick Knight (see opposite, top).

The most successful variation in Kawakubo's 'Body Meets Dress, Dress Meets Body' collection came in Vichy polyester stretch fabric with sewn-in pockets, into which removeable pads could be slipped like the pads in a push-up bra. But here the pads had moved all over the body to the 'wrong' places. Vivienne Westwood had overemphasized female curves through pads in her 'Vive la Cocotte' collection of Autumn/Winter 1995–96 (see opposite, bottom right). This almost grotesque overemphasis – super-large bust, round bottom and hips, slim waist – drew attention to the artificial construction of femininity. Kawakubo did the same, but by crassly disfiguring the erotic female silhouette rather than overdrawing it. Here the traditional construction of femininity slipped out of place: the hip pads, for example, migrated to the front, while the breast pads, enormously enlarged, floated to the back, lending the whole the inflated hunchback appearance that the press were quick to note (see opposite, bottom left). On the back of this disfigurement, a new graceful silhouette came into being. The new shape, as witty as it was sometimes captivatingly beautiful, put the construction of the ideal woman's body on display by radically and literally displacing traditional Western, 'padded' femininity.

The success of Japanese designers on the European and American scene, accompanied by cries of outrage, was, then, not just the result of diversification in a global age, with authentic Japanese labels establishing themselves alongside French, Italian or English equivalents. Authenticity is, in any case, a tricky concept in Japan: the traditional kimono, for example, was in fact the result of Chinese influence in Japan during the fifth century. Following an imperial decree at the beginning of the twentieth century, men employed in the service of the state – policemen, teachers and railway officials, for example – were ordered to wear Western clothing. Army and school uniforms soon followed suit. By the mid-1930s, Japanese clothing for women was also almost entirely Westernized. Eventually most women did it *comme des garçons* – 'going West' even without imperial decree. The kimono is today a folkloric relic, similar to national costumes in Bavaria or Scotland. What mattered to Miyake, Yamamoto and Kawakubo was to decode and recode Western fashion, which, by imperial decree, was also their fashion: the empire designs back.

The question is how, in their systematic radicalism, these designers managed to achieve this decoding and recoding of the established ideas of fashion with such outstanding success. The answer might be that the displacement of convention is the secret of every great designer. Fashion at its best deconstructs the systems that it has itself created. It pursues, to borrow from Friedrich Nietzsche, the re-evaluation of all values.[4] Fashion is not a game without limits but a game with its own self-imposed limits; a disruption dependent on a set of rules. Haute couture, which developed as a commentary on the limits set by and through clothes, is a discourse in clothes about clothes and the displacement of boundaries of gender and class established by clothes. Fashion is nothing other than this crossing of boundaries.

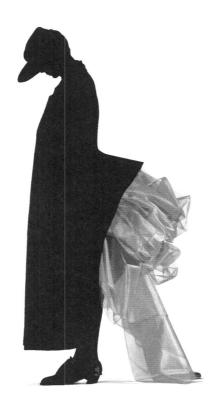

Coco Chanel's work is a particularly good illustration of this crossing of boundaries, since her strategy was to dress women *comme des garçons* and to transfer English into French. Speaking of herself in the third person, she is said to have told Salvador Dalí that 'She took the English masculine and made it feminine. All her life, she did nothing but make women's clothes from men's clothes: jackets, haircuts, ties and cufflinks.'[5] Godfather to this new woman influenced by masculinity was not the bourgeois gentleman but the dandy, an English aristocratic figure whom Charles Baudelaire celebrated as the 'black prince of elegance', and whom Chanel advised women to emulate in the way they wore their clothes.[6] Her rival, the designer Paul Poiret, referred derisively to this nonchalance – the carefully cultivated appearance of not giving any thought to the clothes one is wearing – and to the 'deluxe poverty' of Chanel's clothes. All this might feature in the handbook of the perfect dandy. Yves Saint Laurent's tuxedo of the 1970s is the last link in a long chain of the appropriation of the dandy's dress by women's fashion.

If the Japanese succeeded so magnificently in disfiguring and refiguring the fashion system, it is because they looked on Western fashion from a different perspective. The designers from Tokyo were able to draw on a wealth of alternative sartorial encodings of the relationship between the sexes, as well as on a fundamentally different play between body and fabric. For example, while the décolleté was the classic female erotic zone in Europe until the nineteenth century, in Japan it was the back of the neck. Yamamoto's white felt dress of the Autumn/Winter 1996–97 collection exposes the neck as the erotic zone par excellence (see opposite, top).

The moulding of the body through clothes, through padding and lacing, for example, which is so central to European fashion, is not the aim of the kimono. What is sought is a multi-layered look, which never can nor should fit like a glove. The eroticization of the female body therefore follows a completely different pattern: the kimono gives prominence to the space between the fabric and the body. When Miyake makes the space between body and fabric the subject of his clothes, he is playing with a locus that does not exist in Western fashion. We speak of the dress as a 'second skin'. If the dress is not figure-hugging, the fabric must be sufficiently transparent to reveal the form beneath, just as draped or softly falling clothes swirl around the body the better to emphasize its shape. Even in the two-dimensional dresses of the 1960s, such as those of André Courrèges, the contours of the body can be guessed at through movement or through peepholes that offer sudden glimpses. For Miyake, in contrast, since the space between the dress and the body is where fashion takes place, his trademark has become pleats ironed into the fabric (see opposite, bottom). This pleat drastically changes the dimensions of the dress, making the fabric project from the body. Without any naturalism, it is totally a-mimetic. Nothing suggests the shape of the body, so that, in movement, the dress goes beyond the normal dynamic of concealing and revealing to become a surprising and sophisticated, wholly abstract rhythmic sculpture.

Miyake also makes reference to Japanese traditions through a lack of intervention with the fabric. The idea of fit does not exist with the kimono because the measure is always the length of material, which remains whole and is not cut to size, sewn or fitted to the body using buttons or zips but is instead wrapped around the body and adjusted using a cord or ribbon-like sash, the *obi*, which over time has emancipated itself from its function and turned into a conspicuous accessory. For sumo wrestlers, whose dimensions exceed the standard measure and who like to wear traditional kimonos, extra-wide lengths of material are woven. 'A-POC' (from 'A Piece of Cloth' and a play on 'epoch'), Miyake's collection from 1999, adopted this tradition of the length of material: tubes of fabric were sold uncut – albeit now made from stretch fabric, so they would always fit – pre-embossed with the perforated outline of a garment (see pages 81–83). It is such reference to Japanese tradition that creates appeal in a European context, but these references become fashion only because Japanese fashion sustains a dialogue with Western ideas of fashion, thereby creating tension. Above all, the fundamentally different relationship between the fabric and the body in Japanese fashion brings home European ideals of fashion.

Negative Aesthetics

Over thirty years on the international stage, Rei Kawakubo has deconstructed the central ideals of Western fashion just as systematically and wittily as Issey Miyake and Yohji Yamamoto. It was not for nothing that she chose Paris in which to launch her label internationally, as well as giving it a French name. Until the early 1970s, Paris's claim as the capital of fashion was so absolute that it is difficult for us to imagine today. But orientalism was part of a very French tradition, from Poiret to Yves Saint Laurent. The clothes of Hanae Mori, the grande dame of Japanese fashion before Kawakubo, could not be more Parisian, but had a touch of orientalism. In 1977 she became the first Asian woman to be admitted as an official haute couture designer to the Fédération française de la couture, du prêt-à-porter des couturiers et des créateurs de mode.

Kawakubo's Comme des Garçons proclaimed cross-dressing as a fundamental principle, for which she sacrificed her own name in an industry where the making of a name is everything. Kawakubo, who asserts that she does not speak any European languages, claims that she just liked the sound of the words of the French singer Françoise Hardy's song of 1962, 'Tous les garçons et les filles', which she heard by chance. Whatever the case, by assuming this name, Kawakubo was distancing herself from the work of Mori, whose fashion was the epitome of femininity, and putting herself in the tradition of Chanel, who famously saw the secret of her success in dressing women as *garçons*, and thereby finally dressing them naturally.

Like Mori, Kawakubo continued to take Western fashion as her point of reference, but the manner of reference was radically different from Mori's. Over-fulfilling Western norms, Mori's clothes sought to be more feminine, more elegant and more perfect than those of the Parisian couturiers. To be more Parisian than the Parisians was her secret ideal. Kawakubo, in contrast, exposed the norms that determined Western and thus Parisian fashion by subverting and transgressing them. She iconoclastically questioned one of the unwritten axioms of Western culture: the French monopoly on elegance and the expertise of the French couturiers. The focus of her challenge was the 'Western woman' as the ideal of beauty, sex appeal and grace.

To knock the figure of Mori from her pedestal, Kawakubo worked systematically not only at redefining the relationship between dress and body but also at recoding the associations attached to noble and expensive and lowly and poor fabrics, examining the idea of perfection and reconsidering the relationship between revealing and concealing – that is, the code used to eroticize the body. The cleverly devised asymmetry of her clothes, the loose layering and the mistakes consciously woven into her fabrics, branded the idea of the perfect cut, the absolute line and faultless execution as relics from a bygone age. The black pullovers of the 'Lace' collection (Autumn/Winter 1982–83), strewn arbitrarily with holes as if eaten by an army of moths, seemed to come straight from the baggage of a homeless lady. This now legendary collection made an ironic commentary on the most sophisticated arts of embroidery and lacemaking, without failing to attain their sophistication. Kawakubo's elevation of the bag lady to a new ideal must have sent a shiver down the spines of those powerful elites who adhere unremittingly to the ostentatious display of Western values through wealth.[7]

The shock that Kawakubo's fashion provoked was not primarily social shock, however. Her aesthetic is not principally the aesthetic of poverty, even if this contributes to its provocative impact: it is a negative aesthetic, an examination of our idea of fashion itself. As Harold Koda has shown, it is influenced by the ascetic ideals of Zen Buddhism, which evolved in the sixteenth and seventeenth centuries in opposition to the protocol, ceremony and ostentation of court life.[8] It might be claimed that Kawakubo draws on the charisma and aesthetic characteristics of such religious movements, as Akiko Fukai has shown using the example of *wabi-sabi* – a Japanese world view based on the aesthetics of the incomplete and the faulty.[9]

But how Japanese is such an aesthetic? The West, too, is undoubtedly familiar with poverty or sparsity as an aesthetic category opposed to the lustre and false appearances of the vain world, instead promoting such ideals as asceticism, self-sufficiency, freedom from desire, and solitude from the disruptive hustle and bustle of the world. In the French *Ancien Régime*, the anti-aesthetics of the Parisian religious reform movement of the seventeenth century, the Jansenists at Port-Royal, laid the foundations for an aesthetic appreciation of poverty, age and signs of wear and tear, of coldness, darkness and decay. It is an acknowledgment of the non-beautiful, a making legible of the traces of a truth that has been whitewashed over by the ideal of beauty, an articulation of the fallen nature and mortality of an only apparently beautiful world.

According to the German philosopher Georg Wilhelm Friedrich Hegel, Western aesthetics have, since Christian times, not regarded art as the sensual representation of God's perfection. Hegel maintained that, since the kenosis of Christ on the cross was the matrix of Romantic art – that is, art in the age of Christianity – the truth of European art lay no longer in perfect beauty but rather in the imperfect and defective. The supersensuous perfection of the divine is necessarily missed in the perfectly beautiful.[10] This division between sensual appearance and the transcendent reality of the depicted is manifested in an aesthetic of the un-ideal that becomes particularly striking in the art of the portrait. An example is the warts depicted so prominently by Piero della Francesca on the profile of Federico da Montefeltro in one of the most famous portraits of the Renaissance (1466, Galleria degli Uffizi, Florence). Such an aesthetic of the un-ideal individual, the defective and the imperfect, also surfaced in Western fashion: Coco Chanel, for example, used cotton rib, a 'low' material from which workers' clothes were made, for haute couture. Martin Margiela continued this trend and – in a dialogue with Kawakubo – took it to its peak. Thus once again, Kawakubo's clothes are cutting-edge not only because they embody a Japanese aesthetic but also because they enter into a dialogue with Western fashion practices as part of the realization of this aesthetic.

For the French literary theorist and philosopher Roland Barthes, the *érotisme* of Western female fashion lies in the rhetoric of the gap: 'Is not the most erotic portion of the body where the garment gapes?'[11] This peekaboo voyeurism is not the rhetoric of Kawakubo, who negates the erotic tropes of Western fashion. In her clothes, the West can learn to read bodies anew: instead of the dialectic of concealing and revealing and the associated conventions of sexuality, a new sensuality emerges in the depth of layered fabrics and changing lines. Freed from Western erotic conventions, the thoroughly sensual wit of these clothes is all the more striking. Rarely has an intercultural change of context released such an aesthetic power so suddenly.

Jean Paul Gaultier wittily exposed the sexual showing-off at the heart of Western fashion. An essential part of this bravado is the division of the body into fetish-like objects and the enlargement and isolation of particular parts: breasts, waist, feet and so on. These parts of the body are then constricted in their freedom of movement to become eye-catchers, becoming accessories, exhibited in and of themselves. A whole new set of mechanics is created – how to sit down in a short, tight skirt, how to walk in high heels – in order to keep the tension between concealing and revealing alive. Against such an erotic staging of the body, Kawakubo posits a body that is not exhibited to the gaze, but rather protected, allowed to remain whole and moveable. Her work deconstructs the Western opposition between nudity and clothes, and promotes in its place a symbiosis of clothes and body. This fashion is strongly physical. It does not, however, treat the body as an object to be exhibited, but rather as something intimate. What is at stake is neither the sublimation nor the hiding away of the body but rather a new mode of embodiment.

A Dress

One dress by Kawakubo can serve as an example: the evening dress from her collection for Autumn/Winter 1984–85, which picks up a theme that could not be more Western – that of the classical statue, and, more specifically, the female torso covered in gauzy drapery (see overleaf). With her silks cut on the bias, the French couturier Madeleine Vionnet (1876–1975) came closest to making this classicist ideal reality in the twentieth century. The body shimmered as promisingly through the folds of her fabric as it did through the apparently effortlessly worked marble of the ancients (see page 37). Kawakubo's evening dress, however, strikes at the core of the Greek inheritance and all subsequent classicisms. It exemplifies her disturbing reinterpretation, her taking apart and reconfiguring of the fashion system. A signature piece, the now over twenty-five-year-old dress embodies her poetics and can be read as a *pars pro toto* for the strategies she subsequently developed. Through a defamiliarizing reading of classical antiquity, it is a skilful and witty commentary on the idea of veiling the body and, thus, on one of the central tenets of Western eroticism: the tension between nudity and concealment. For Kawakubo does not veil the body: she wraps it up; she packages it. By rewriting the Western history of classicism, she reveals the relationship between the nude, the naked and the dressed in a new light.

Kawakubo's evening gown displays in great style her characteristic near-aggressive modesty, which to the superficial gaze might be mistaken for mere raggedness. Our expectations of an evening dress are systematically rebuffed. The very idea of a 'civilized' dress is slapped in the face. It should be remembered that, until the 1980s, the length of skirt, measured to the nearest centimetre, was perhaps the most important feature of the seasonal change in fashion. To be considered fashionable, it was absolutely crucial to have the correct length of skirt. But to speak of a dress length here would be frivolous. The seam is asymmetrical, tapering to points. The principle of the seam is taken up again in the collar, which is similarly asymmetrical, tapering triangularly at the front and in more rectangular fashion at the back. The gown is also made from the 'wrong' fabric and is the 'wrong' colour: rather than being cut from a shimmering, supple, colourful material or from elegant black silk, it is of charcoal-grey, fine-knit wool jersey – a material in which to work, not party. But that is not the worst of it.

Rei Kawakubo/Comme des Garçons
Autumn/Winter 1984–85
Photograph by Peter Lindbergh

Madeleine Vionnet
Silk crêpe romaine pyjamas, *c.* 1931
Photograph by George Hoyningen-Huene

Maenad
Roman copy (120–149 CE) of Greek relief
of the end of the fifth century BCE

The dress appears to be made from two pieces, since above the tunic undergarment, the fabric lies in horizontal folds. It has been created from the fusion of two classical types. The strong emphasis of the line underneath the buttocks, which defines the lower limit of the torso, is characteristic of a particular type of Aphrodite figure, known to archaeologists as the Venus Anadyomene, whose naked upper body emerges from drapes of fabric. The other type that the dress evokes is the Roman goddess Ceres, typically depicted wearing a doubled cloth himation with horizontal drapery over the torso and vertical drapery on the lower body, her leg carefully posed with the knee pressing forward from under the fabric. But Kawakubo's drapery does not let anything show through. This brings us to the worst.

Western classicisms of all kinds are given a rough time by Kawakubo's evening dress. It mocks the sex appeal of Western clothes. In Kawakubo's work, the torso, which emerges naked in the Anadyomene, is emphasized by the dynamic spiral of the upward movement of the fabric. Yet Kawakubo's dress does not allow any flesh to shimmer seductively through: it wraps the body. Thus the art of classic European tailoring, with its focus on elaborate revealing and veiling, is skilfully surpassed to achieve an opposite result. Through a completely new technique of drapery on the body, with invisible seams and stitching, gravity is outwitted. This technique holds the fabric in place; it cannot swirl around the body. Where, in antiquity, high art was demonstrated by the ability to create the effect of textiles in marble and stone, here the quality of the work is shown in the textile imitation of stone; the transformation of stone into veils is undone through a petrifaction of the fabric. The dress thus deliberately and satirically subverts the eminently classical theme of the sheer veil.

In this way, Kawakubo brings the dialectic of stone and flesh to its climax. Her dress becomes stone so that, instead of stiffening into a classical marble statue, the body, naked under its wrappings, is allowed to come alive. Paradoxically, this technique of wrapping the body in stone releases it from its marble nudity, making it warm, mobile and sensual – naked under the drapery. By setting aside the old notion of sex appeal, Kawakubo creates a new eroticism that is at least partly the product of the freedom of movement enjoyed by women in this dress in contrast to the classic evening dress. The woman is no longer a passive exhibition piece and can, *comme des garçons*, do karate or leap into a taxi while still maintaining her allure.

The empire has designed back – with a vengeance.

1. See Ingrid Loschek, *When Clothes Become Fashion: Design and Innovation Systems*, Oxford (Berg) 2009.

2. See Yuniya Kawamura, *The Japanese Revolution in Paris Fashion*, Oxford (Berg) 2004.

3. See Salman Rushdie, 'The Empire Writes Back – With a Vengeance', in Bill Ashcroft, Gareth Griffiths, Helen Tifflin, *The Empire Writes Back: Theory and Practice in Post-Colonial Literatures*, London and New York (Routledge) 1989. Rushdie was punning on the title of one of the *Star Wars* films: *The Empire Strikes Back*. 'Writing back' is used to describe a post-colonial form of intertextuality in which the Western canon is rewritten and thereby subtly disfigured and displaced.

4. Shortly after his death Friedrich Nietzsche's sister collected his last unpublished writings under the title *The Will to Power*. Nietzsche had considered using this title for a work he was writing, but later abandoned it in favour of *Revaluation of All Values*, which he was unable to complete before his death.

5. Quoted in André Parinaud, *The Unspeakable Confessions of Salvador Dalí*, New York (Morrow) 1981, p. 212, as cited by Valerie Steele in *Women of Fashion: Twentieth-Century Designers*, New York (Rizzoli) 1991, p. 41.

6. See Valerie Steele and Jennifer Park, *Gothic: Dark Glamour*, New Haven, Conn., and London (Yale University Press) 2008, p. 30.

7. See Rei Kawakubo, 'The Top 25', *W*, 2–9 December 1983, p. 61; Harold Koda, 'Rei Kawakubo and the Aesthetic of Poverty', *Dress*, vol. 11 (1985), pp. 5–10.

8. Koda 1985.

9. Akiko Fukai, 'Le Japon et la mode' in *XXIème CIEL: Mode in Japan*, ed. Marie-Pierre Foissy-Aufrère, Nice (Musée des Arts Asiatiques) and Milan (5 Continents) 2003, pp. 22–23.

10. Georg Wilhelm Friedrich Hegel, *Vorlesungen über die Ästhetik*, ed. Max Bense, Stuttgart (Walther) 1968.

11. Roland Barthes, *The Pleasure of Text*, trans. Richard Miller, London (Blackwell) 1990, pp. 9–10.

IN PRAISE OF SHADOWS

During the 1980s, as the world's gaze turned to Japan's economic growth and success, attention also focused on the country's fashion, which offered a set of formal and aesthetic values completely different from those held by the West.

The pioneering efforts of such designers as Kenzo Takada and Issey Miyake in the 1970s were followed by Rei Kawakubo and Yohji Yamamoto, who showed in Paris for the first time in 1981. Their now legendary Spring/Summer 1983 collections featured black, asymmetric, deconstructed, artfully ripped and unravelled garments. These clothes represented a complete departure from Western pattern-cutting traditions and rejected the body-consciousness obsession then current in fashion. The collections were unlike anything else on the catwalk at the time and ignited furious debate in the international fashion community.

Kawakubo's and Yamamoto's offerings may have been thoughtlessly dubbed the 'beggar look', but the so-called black rags were calculated in their design – the expression of an aesthetic at ease with untidiness and imperfection. Fashion during the early 1980s, arguably led by French designer Yves Saint Laurent, was all about colour, and plenty of it. The Japanese designers, however, deliberately avoided vivid colours and made heavy use of a monochromatic palette, from strong and varied hues of black to the simplicity and crispness of shades of white. Henceforth, Japanese fashion was not only perceived as unstructured and dishevelled; it also became synonymous with the colour black and stark, monochrome minimalism.

Kawakubo's and Yamamoto's black was often an unassuming, harmonious shade, reminiscent of Japanese ink painting. Their expressive use of a black palette also partook of the qualities celebrated in Juni'chirō Tanizaki's book *In Praise of Shadows* (1933), which finds in shadow the essence of the Japanese aesthetic and speaks of the Japanese skill with light and shade (see page 49).

The designers' choice of colour, unfettered by any Western paradigm, was perceptively singled out by the *Washington Post* as the distinguishing feature of their style, along with the purity of their aesthetic.[1] The French newspaper *Libération* likened Kawakubo's and Yamamoto's creations to the intense black-and-white films of Kenji Mizoguchi, while French *Vogue* compared them to calligraphy scrolls, which symbolize a beauty devoid of colour.[2]

Black has always been ambiguous. It has a wealth of potent meanings: power, sex or poverty, for example; and, in many cultures, it is the colour of death and mourning. It is often the expression of an age: the paintings of Diego Velázquez record the opulent black attire of seventeenth-century Spanish aristocrats. Designers Coco Chanel, Christian Dior and Cristóbal Balenciaga employed black to great effect for their most elegant outfits, using it to reinforce demure sophistication, striking silhouettes and simple lines. In contrast, Left Bank existentialists, American beat poets, elegant gothic dandies and punks wore black to express disaffection with societal norms or as a protest against the Establishment. Playing on these associations, Kawakubo and Yamamoto chose stoical black as the strongest tool for their expression. The designers radically reduced all elements to zero and used black to accentuate the silhouette.

Rei Kawakubo/Comme des Garçons
Spring/Summer 1983
Photograph by Peter Lindbergh

The dramatic effect of black and white is seen clearly in photographs of Rei Kawakubo's work in the 1980s by Hans Feurer and by Peter Lindbergh (see opposite). The images capture perfectly the light and shade generated by the textures, and the looseness and the layering of fabric. Kawakubo, for her part, claims to see myriad hues in black. In her Autumn/Winter collection from 1988–89, however, she declared 'Red is Black' and was exposed as the master of a rather more varied colour palette. Occasionally she returns to black, producing free-spirited and powerful designs that somehow impress the fact that black is made of all the colours of the spectrum.

Yohji Yamamoto makes contemporary clothing that incorporates quintessential elements of menswear design and offers distillations of couture elegance. He makes frequent use of black as an 'intellectual', 'contemporary' and 'luxury' colour and, since 1995, has made a line of clothing called 'Noir'.[3] While he has evoked many moods through black over the years, each season he nonetheless produces pieces that are utterly of the moment.

In the late twentieth century, the new black of these two designers inspired many of their contemporaries to follow suit, making it the colour of the age. Black was widely adopted by such Western designers as Martin Margiela and Ann Demeulemeester. The latest generation of Japanese designers, including Junya Watanabe, Jun Takahashi of Undercover and Hiroyuki Horihata and Makiko Sekiguchi of Matohu, are also highly attuned to the power of black. Watanabe uses black head to toe in recent collections (see pages 59–60); Takahashi's frayed patchwork creations are enhanced by different textiles in varying shades of black, brown and blue (see page 58); and Matohu's brand of contemporary kimono has seen the intense use of a deep blue-black with delicate flecks of gold (see page 57). Japanese fashion continues to take the multilayered symbolism of black and use it to add depth and meaning to modern fashion.

1. Nina Hyde, 'Japan's Runway Look', *Washington Post*, 16 October 1982.
2. Claire Mises, 'Prêt-à-Porter 1982', *Libération*, 17–18 October 1981; 'Le Soleil se lève sur la Mode Japonaise' (The Sun Rises on Japanese Fashion), French *Vogue*, no. 631 (November 1982).
3. Yohji Yamamoto interviewed by Akiko Fukai in *WOWOW* television programme, Tokyo, 19 November 2002.

Rei Kawakubo/Comme des Garçons
Spring/Summer 1983
Off-white cotton jersey blouse with cotton ribbon appliqué; washed white patchwork dress of sheeting and rayon satin

'The creation of the fabric is 80% of the work involved in making the overall garment.'[1]
This oversized, asymmetrical and torn blouse and dress are a typical example of Rei Kawakubo's collections from the early 1980s, which were dominated by the use of a simple, monochromatic palette. Kawakubo eloquently expresses a world of nuanced shadow using four different types of white fabric, which hang loosely on the body, creating soft drapes and folds. The blouse's creased cotton appliquéd ribbons give an uneven texture and emphasize the garment's distressed and ragged qualities – features born out of the designer's enduring experimentation with fabrics deliberately treated at the point of production to appear aged or flawed. The aesthetic of Kawakubo's early collections, together with those of Yohji Yamamoto, was derisively referred to by some fashion writers at the time as the 'beggar look' or the 'Japanese bag-lady look'.

1. Rei Kawakubo quoted in Yoko Sato, 'The creation of the fabric is 80% of the work involved in making the overall garment', *Asahi Shimbun*, 22 November 1982, p. 15.

Rei Kawakubo/Comme des Garçons
Spring/Summer 1983
Photograph by Peter Lindbergh

Rei Kawakubo/Comme des Garçons
Autumn/Winter 1983–84
Black wool knitted sweater; black wool/
nylon skirt

Rei Kawakubo presented another range of black garments for Comme des Garçons in Autumn/Winter 1983–84. This sweater is a complex assemblage of irregularly braided wide-knit panels that twist and swirl around the torso. Its distorted, undulating form produces subtle surface shadows, exaggerating the sweater's voluminous appearance.

The sweater's wearer is, one imagines, assertive and, like Kawakubo, in search of a beauty of which she herself can be convinced. 'The woman who wears

Comme des Garçons is', according to Holly Brubach, writing in the *Atlantic Monthly* in 1984, 'unwilling to dress herself up so that other people have something pleasing to look at.'[1]

The word *karasu-zoku* ('the crow gang') was regularly applied to groups of black-clad men and women in Japan at this time.

1. Holly Brubach, 'The Truth in Fiction', *Atlantic Monthly*, May 1984, p. 96. Cited in Harold Koda, 'Rei Kawakubo and the Aesthetic of Poverty', *Costume*, no. 11, 1985.

Rei Kawakubo/Comme des Garçons
Spring/Summer 1984
Black linen dress, gathered with rubber belt

Yohji Yamamoto
Spring/Summer 1983
Photograph by Hiroshi Sugimoto

Why should this propensity to seek beauty in darkness be so strong only in Orientals? The West too has known a time when there was no electricity, gas, or petroleum, and yet so far as I know the West has never been disposed to delight in shadows. Japanese ghosts have traditionally had no feet; Western ghosts have feet, but are transparent. As even this trifle suggests, pitch darkness has always occupied our fantasies, while in the West even ghosts are as clear as glass. This is true too of our household implements: we prefer colours compounded of darkness, they prefer the colours of sunlight. And of silver and copperware: we love them for the burnish and patina, which they consider unclean, insanitary, and polish to a glittering brilliance. They paint their ceilings and walls in pale colours to drive out as many of the shadows as they can. We fill our gardens with dense plantings, they spread out a flat expanse of grass.

But what produces such differences in taste? In my opinion it is this: we Orientals tend to seek our satisfactions in whatever surroundings we happen to find ourselves, to content ourselves with things as they are; and so darkness causes us no discontent, we resign ourselves to it as inevitable. If light is scarce then light is scarce; we will immerse ourselves in the darkness and there discover its own particular beauty.

Juni'chirō Tanizaki, In Praise of Shadows *(1933)*[1]

1. Excerpt from Juni'chirō Tanizaki, *In Praise of Shadows* [1933], trans. Thomas J. Harper and Edward G. Seidensticker, London (Vintage) 2001, pp. 47–48.

Yohji Yamamoto
Spring/Summer 1983
Above: White cotton plain-weave cut-work
jacket and dress
Opposite: White cotton plain-weave cut-
work dress and trousers

Yohji Yamamoto's unique attitude towards design and his desire to push forward new concepts of beauty have always been intertwined with a sense of everyday life and the real world: 'If one has only one piece of clothing in life, it becomes patched together, exposed to sun and rain, frayed from the course of daily life. I wanted to create clothing with the same kind of unconscious beauty and natural appeal.'[1]

These loose-fitting cotton garments are riddled with holes, carefully cut and finished in stylized patterns, some floral and some abstract. Soft shadows, like dappled sunlight, are cast on to the garment and the wearer's skin, yielding a subtle sensuality and the natural, unconscious beauty to which Yamamoto aspired.

Yamamoto's Spring/Summer 1983 collection, like Rei Kawakubo's, featured simple unstructured, asymmetric garments in natural tones, offering a new, modest aesthetic that rejected mainstream European taste, which was characterized in the brash 1980s by bold, sculpted silhouettes and body consciousness – the antithesis of the authentic beauty Yamamoto sought to define.

1. Quoted in Sato 1982.

Yohji Yamamoto
Autumn/Winter 1993–94
Black wool serge dress with stitching
in white string
Photograph by Hiroshi Sugimoto

Rei Kawakubo/Comme des Garçons
Spring/Summer 2009
Black synthetic 'leather' top and skirt

Hairstyling sketchbook by Julien d'Ys
for Rei Kawakubo/Comme des Garçons
Spring/Summer 2009

Yohji Yamamoto
Autumn/Winter 2009–10
Black wool melton coat; black silk
georgette trousers

Yohji Yamamoto captures the very essence
of early twentieth-century men's clothing
– as seen in the poised black-and-white
photographs by August Sander that he so
admires – and makes it the foundation
of his work. It is also in deference to this
source that the designer's reduced palette is
typically black, punctuated here and there,
as in this collection, with white or red.

Yamamoto applies these elements to elegant
contemporary garments that superbly express
the complexity of the modern woman.
    This ensemble of melton coat and
trousers complete with an Inverness-style
cape encapsulates Yamamoto's mastery of
traditional tailoring with a twist: except for
the collar, all the garment's edges have been
deliberately left unfinished.

Matohu
Autumn/Winter 2009–10
Blue-black wool/rayon/polyester coat;
dark blue polyester jacquard dress; leather
belt with studs

The twisting gold lamé thread in this bluish-
black coat is evocative of the sky in the early
evening or a night of twinkling stars. It is a

contemporary reference to the layering
techniques of the kimono, and is from a
collection by Matohu called 'Kabuki-mono'
– a reference to outlandish, non-conformist
sixteenth-century samurai warriors whose
dress was daring and flamboyant.

Matohu, formed by the duo Hiroyuki
Horihata and Makiko Sekiguchi, presented
their debut collection in Tokyo in 2005. They

take inspiration from the beauty and traditions
of the Keicho Period (1596–1615), during
which Japanese culture matured dramatically.
The designers express the sensitive beauty of
that era through a revival and reinterpretation
of traditional printing and dyeing techniques,
decorative motifs, silhouettes and, in this
'Kabuki-mono' collection, a dark and rich
palette fused with a modern-day punk attitude.

Jun Takahashi/Undercover
Spring/Summer 2006
Dark blue linen coat, lined with brown
cotton pile fabric and trimmed with
circular printed cotton jersey fabrics;
dark blue cotton jersey tube top; skirt
remade from a printed fabric

Junya Watanabe/Junya Watanabe Comme des Garçons
Autumn/Winter 2008–09
Black wool jersey dress

Junya Watanabe/
Junya Watanabe Comme des Garçons
Autumn/Winter 2009–10
Black nylon taffeta coat with polyester
padding and golden metal chain; black
wool knit dress with gold print

Junya Watanabe's 'Feather and Air'
collection transformed casual down coats
into elegant contemporary garments and
shone the spotlight not on the purpose of
such a jacket to protect the wearer from the
cold but instead on its lightness and volume.
Despite functional overtones, the dramatic
and romantic form of this coat makes it
appear to be from a bygone era.

Watanabe's skilful play with the light-
reflecting surfaces peculiar to synthetic
fabrics confirms the garment as current
and modern, however. When the collection
was presented on the catwalk, the models
emerged from the shadows, flashes of gold
chain and one stark white blouse providing
the only moments of disruption to the black
on black of the collection.

Scrapbook by fashion observer/illustrator
Lele Acquarone published in Italian *Vogue*,
October 2009

FLATNESS

While power dressing was the order of the day in Europe and America in the early 1980s, Japanese fashion had a reputation for shapelessness and reduction. Journalists were often critical in their responses to the designers' work at this time. Behind their disapprobation was not only astonishment and incredulity at such an audacious assault on fashion, but also a cultural divide in the conception of clothing. Western dressmaking took the natural shape of the human body as a given, and its objective was to produce a solution to the challenge of contouring a three-dimensional form using two-dimensional fabric. By contrast, Japanese designers' creations shrouded the body: they used huge swathes of fabric to wrap and envelop the human form – a strategy of concealment and camouflage that, the critic Deyan Sudjic has argued, deliberately avoided conventional notions of gender in dress.[1] Their garments concealed the curvaceous bosom, narrow waist and natural proportions of the female shape.

It is probably not wrong to assume that deep in the mind of every Japanese person lies the culture of kimono. In the making of a kimono, an uncut length of fabric is put on the human body, resulting in an excess of fabric that creates drapes. The Japanese see this excess as *ma* (roughly translated as 'space') and never consider it illegitimate. The Japanese designers' baggy, shapeless dresses were also, in many cases, asymmetric – another core element of Japanese aesthetics. Their designs demonstrated a universal approach to clothing, breaking down the barriers of gender, age and body shape just as a kimono does.

Issey Miyake confronted the world with the concept of modern two-dimensional clothing in 1976 when he unveiled his 'A Piece of Cloth' concept, which wrapped the moving body in a single length of fabric. 'A Piece of Cloth' presented a new take on clothing design, capitalizing on the versatility of *ma* to transcend physical differences and achieve an abstract relationship with the body. These concepts are most visible in Miyake's collaboration with renowned American photographer Irving Penn, which started in 1986; Penn's interpretation of Miyake's experiments with line and mass creates strikingly sculptural and often vividly coloured abstract photographs. These deceptively simple images belie the technical complexity involved in achieving Miyake's designs.

Miyake combined his reductive approach with the sophisticated technical capabilities of Japan's synthetic-fibre industry. In 1988 the designer presented the 'Pleats' series, a range of functional garments made from pleated polyester, refined and released to commercial production as the 'Pleats Please' line in 1993. Hugely successful with women of all ages and body types because of its flattering lines, comfort, ease of care and timeless style, 'Pleats Please' is the range with which Miyake has become synonymous.

In 1999 Miyake went on to launch the 'A-POC' collection (a term coined from 'A Piece of Cloth' and a play on the word 'epoch'), developed with textile engineer Dai Fujiwara, then designer and now creative director in the Miyake Design Studio. 'A-POC' is a range of tubular knitwear produced on specially adapted Raschel knitting machines, made without machine-sewn seams and finished on a roll. When the roll is unfurled, the garments – stitched into the tube – can be cut free (see pages 80–83). Both 'Pleats Please' and 'A-POC' have garnered global acclaim for their innovative design and functionality and for rising brilliantly to a multiplicity of challenges, including those of production, wearability and portability.

Naoya Hatakeyama's series of graphic images of Rei Kawakubo's (Comme des Garçons) dresses, commissioned by the Kyoto Costume Institute in 2008, capture in stark simplicity the extraordinary shapes of her clothes when unworn (see pages 67–77). From Hatakeyama's photographs it is impossible to discern a garment's pattern, or to predict what it will look like before it is put on and the voluminous shape it will take when worn, or even to establish which holes to put the head or arms through. Revealed in this way, the garments possess a striking geometry and testify to Kawakubo's long interest in asymmetric forms. The designer went on to astound the international fashion community with her so-called 'Lumps and Bumps' collection (Spring/Summer 1997; see pages 31, 163–69) – yet another excellent application of the 'flatness'-inspired notion that clothing need not necessarily trace the contours of the body. Simple yet complex and sometimes completely unfathomable, 'these are clothes made to be worn by the mind as well as the body'.[2]

The absence of a 'constructed' (or tailored) quality – which might be seen to constitute the Western idea of order – could be viewed as a deconstructive act, paradoxically generating its own innate structure. These designers questioned the artifice of tailoring and couture, and introduced the language of deconstruction into the realm of fashion. In the postmodern era of the late twentieth century, such concepts liberated people from existing Western conventions of fashion. From that moment, world fashion, hand in hand with Japanese designers, took its first steps into a new dimension.

1. Deyan Sudjic, 'Japan Style', in *Excess: Fashion and the Underground in the '80s*, ed. Maria Luisa Frisa and Stefano Tonchi, Milan (Edizioni Charta) 2004, p. 398.
2. Bradley Quinn, 'Japanese Innovation', in *Techno Fashion*, Oxford (Berg) 2002, p. 141.

Rei Kawakubo/Comme des Garçons
Autumn/Winter 1992–93
Trained dress of three sheets of black and purplish brown polyester georgette (two sheets at sleeves), black nylon knit at neck

Some ten years on from Rei Kawakubo's 'black shock' debut (see 'In Praise of Shadows', page 41), this collection returned black to prominence. This oversized dress features three shades of black, creating a subtle play of light and shade when the garment is worn. It is made of three layers of diaphanous polyester georgette, extending at the back like a train. This is a garment of extremes and opposites. On the one hand, it drowns its wearer, the tube knit hugging the bodice and shoulders and creeping up the face, while the arms hang, kimono-like, far beyond the fingertips. On the other hand, the sheer layers of the skirt bring exquisite lightness and movement to the piece. Laying the garment flat reveals its striking geometry and asymmetry, as can be seen in the photograph by Naoya Hatakeyama (opposite).

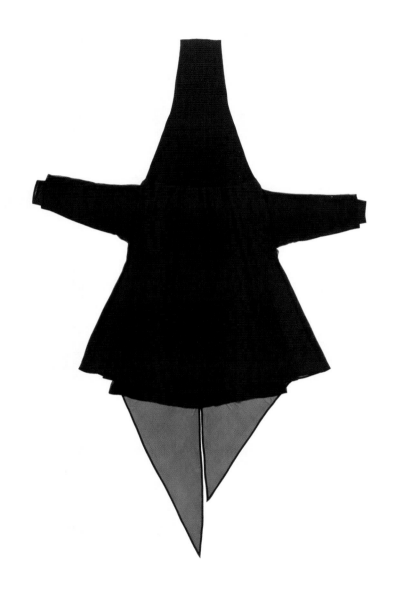

Photograph by Naoya Hatakeyama
2009 Lambda print
Collection of the Kyoto Costume Institute

Rei Kawakubo/Comme des Garçons
Spring/Summer 1998
Dress of twenty sheets of beige binding,
two darts at left side

One large cut was made into a sheaf of binding twenty layers thick to make this dress. A single continuous stitch was then made along the horseshoe-like contour, thereby sealing the layers so they resemble a sleeping bag. The requisite holes for head and arms became slots, and only once worn does the dress pull into shape. What is more, the stitch does not function as a conventional seam: rather, it forms a ridge detail bisecting the garment from front to back, creating an increasingly extravagant ruffle along the bodice.

Photograph by Naoya Hatakeyama
2009 Lambda print
Collection of the Kyoto Costume Institute

Rei Kawakubo/Comme des Garçons
Autumn/Winter 1983–84
Beige wool felt coat; dark blue wool/nylon
flannel skirt

The fifth Comme des Garçons collection to be shown on the Paris catwalk featured several garments that played strongly on the contrast between volume and flatness. When folded, this poncho-like coat creates a geometry of straight lines (see opposite). It is constructed from two rectangular panels, the smaller of which slides through a slit in the larger piece and hangs from the side of the chest. The garment has no buttons or fastenings, and is somewhat reminiscent of traditional Japanese travelling coats, which were made of such affordable materials as paper, and needed to be simple and practical. When worn, the coat is transformed: the excess felt hangs thick and stiff to a point at the front; the slit opens and undulates together with the panels to create an unforeseen dynamic and sculptural volume. The deliberate use of creased and unbleached felt incorporates the Japanese aesthetic principle of *wabi-sabi* (the aesthetics of the incomplete).

Photograph by Naoya Hatakeyama
2009 Lambda print
Collection of the Kyoto Costume Institute

Rei Kawakubo/Comme des Garçons
Autumn/Winter 1983–84
Black rayon jacquard dress with wide rectangular
skirt, trimmed with a panel at centre front, slits
at the upper side of the skirt

The asymmetry, indeterminate forms and
oversized characteristics of Rei Kawakubo's early
work are epitomized beautifully in this dress.
It may appear rather chaotic at first glance, but
the pattern for the garment was created after
exhaustive study of the relationship between
the way the fabric hangs and gravitational force.

Other designers tend to give precise
instructions to their pattern-makers, but at
Comme des Garçons, as journalist Judith
Thurman notes, the process 'begins with a vision,
or perhaps just an intuition, about a key garment
that Kawakubo hints at with a sort of *koan* [a
story or statement]. She gives the patterners a set
of clues that might take the form of a scribble, a
crumpled piece of paper, or an enigmatic phrase
such as "inside-out pillowcase", which they
translate, as best they can, into a muslin – the
three-dimensional blueprint of a garment.
Their first drafts are invariably too concrete.'
The quest continues until the desired results
are achieved: 'The staff calls the process by a
deceptively playful English word, "catchball",'
concludes Thurman.[1]

1. Judith Thurman, 'The Misfit', *New Yorker*, 4 July 2005,
p. 65.

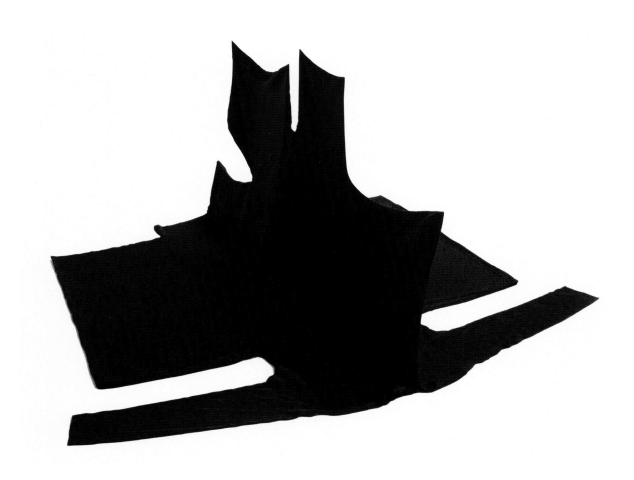

Photograph by Naoya Hatakeyama
2009 Lambda print
Collection of the Kyoto Costume Institute

Rei Kawakubo/Comme des Garçons
Autumn/Winter 1983–84
Black wool jersey dress, with a tube from
front to back and a slit on the tube

This bold graphic shape shows how Rei
Kawakubo devotes the same attention to the
form of a garment when it is lying flat (see
opposite) as when it is worn – a testament
to the extent of her aesthetic sensibility. The
process of putting on this piece is neither
straightforward nor necessarily always the

same. The dress is in the shape of a simple
tube, but a long tubular section runs like a
Möbius strip from the front bodice to the
back to produce an intersecting drape.
Although there are careful instructions on
how to wear the garment, there are in fact
a variety of ways in which the drapes can
be arranged: on or under the shoulders or
along the legs and body, allowing for free
or restricted movement accordingly.
    The designer's affection for making
'clothes that can be manipulated by the

wearer' has been discussed by Deyan Sudjic,
who points out that, while the wearer may not
wish to use the different options, 'the idea that
this is possible affects the way the wearer feels'.
This approach, Sudjic suggests, 'implies that a
garment is not a finite solution, but allows for
an input from the wearer, who plays a part
in shaping the final form. What Kawakubo
offers is a democratic version of high fashion.'[1]

1. Deyan Sudjic, *Rei Kawakubo and Comme des Garçons*,
New York (Rizzoli) 1990, p. 82.

Photograph by Naoya Hatakeyama
2009 Lambda print
Collection of the Kyoto Costume Institute

Rei Kawakubo/Comme des Garçons
Spring/Summer 1984
Grey plain-weave cotton dress, printed
with black brushstroke pattern, with
shirring at neck, left sleeve and right
upper side of the skirt

The bold asymmetry of this garment
represents a fundamental feature in Rei
Kawakubo's work of the early 1980s. Viewed
flat (see opposite), the dress appears as a large
rectangle, out of which a corner has been
cut, the shirring on the left cuff and the
upper edge of the panel further intensifying
the asymmetry. Appearing in three places,

the shirring seems to indicate holes for arms
and head, yet when the dress is worn one of
the three openings cannot be used and hangs
away from the body. The geometry of the
garment is enhanced by the textile's irregular
print, which resembles the bold strokes of
Japanese calligraphy or an expressionistic
painting on canvas.

Photograph by Naoya Hatakeyama
2009 Lambda print
Collection of the Kyoto Costume Institute

Rei Kawakubo/Comme des Garçons
Spring/Summer 1998
Off-white cotton lawn base dress, with the top layer having a print and vinyl coating

A simple, off-white cotton dress is juxtaposed with two pleated tubes – patterned and vinyl-coated – fastened around the bodice and skirt. While its avant-garde appearance challenges notions of comfort and elegance, the garment embodies three traditional Japanese aesthetic principles: the pleats are reminiscent of origami; the frayed edges suggest the spartan approach of *wabi-sabi* (the aesthetics of the incomplete); and the interstices between the pleats and the body represent the rich, potent space known as *ma*. Here the shape of the body is brought into focus not by revealing its contours, as is the convention in the West, but by its absence behind this architectural dress.

Once taken off, the dress can be gathered and given the appearance of a precious gift tied with bows (see opposite).

Issey Miyake
Catwalk presentation of A-POC 'King &
Queen', Spring/Summer 1999
Photographs by Fujitsuka Mitsumasa (top);
Yasuaki Yoshinaga (above)

Opposite: A-POC shown in *Issey Miyake
Making Things* exhibition, Ace Gallery,
New York 1999
Photograph by Yasuaki Yoshinaga

Overleaf: Animation by Pascal Roulin,
Issey Miyake Making Things exhibition,
Fondation Cartier, Paris 1998–99

A-POC

In his endless search for new concepts and modes of production, Issey Miyake returned to the original starting point for his designs. The 'A-POC' collection (combining 'A Piece of Cloth' with a play on the word 'epoch') was launched in 1999, but it represents an idea – what a designer can do with a single piece of fabric – that Miyake has continually explored since the 1970s. Following on from his hugely successful and original take on pleated cloth in the 'Pleats Please' collection launched in 1993, Miyake spent years

researching and developing 'A-POC' in collaboration with textile technologist and designer Dai Fujiwara, currently creative director of the Miyake Design Studio.

Miyake and Fujiwara's innovation was to develop a weaving process that produced fully finished garments without the need for sewing. 'A-POC', in its first incarnation, consisted of long tubes of double-knit fabric with yarns linked in a fine mesh of chain stitches, all produced on a computer-controlled loom. The shape of a dress or skirt, for example,

was embedded into the fabric, leaving the wearer to remove their clothes from the tube by cutting along the marked lines (see overleaf). When the garments were cut free, the bottom, stretchier layer of mesh would shrink and stop the fabric from unravelling.

The revolutionary 'A-POC' concept (how to weave finished clothes, not just fabric) pioneered by Miyake and Fujiwara has enormous potential not only for fashion and textile manufacturing but also for other design disciplines.

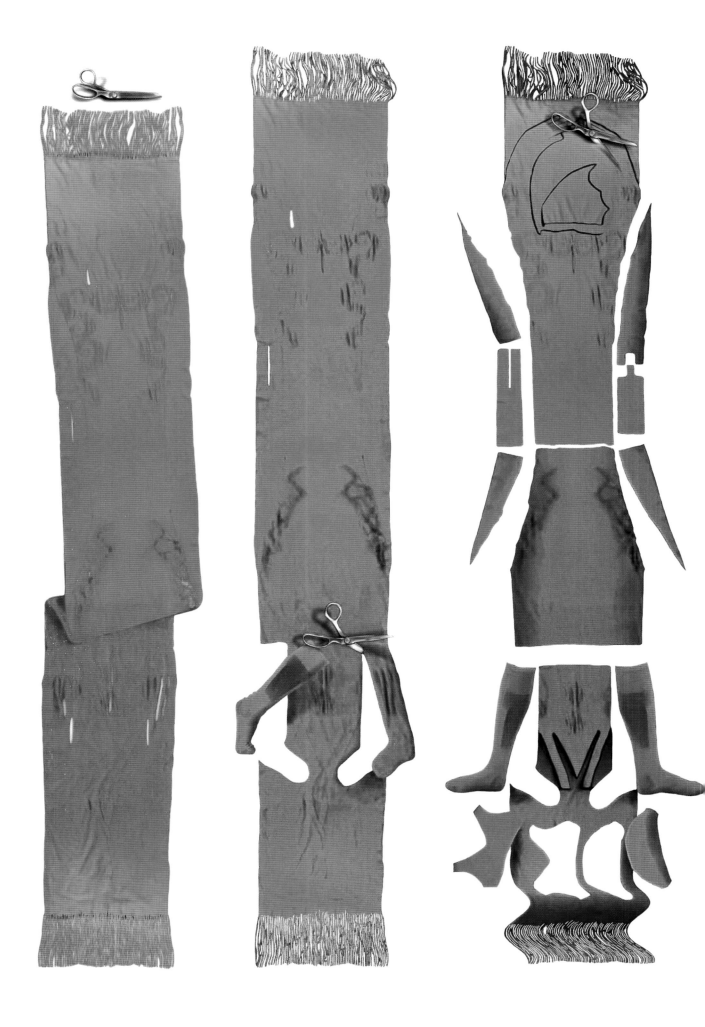

TRADITION AND INNOVATION

Japanese fashion broke new ground when it appeared on the world stage in the early 1980s. Its love affair with black and use of innovative construction techniques combined with a conceptual approach overturned Western ideas of beauty and form. But one thing almost universally acknowledged during this period, even among those less than enamoured with the clothing, was the astute sensibility of Japanese designers when it came to fabric.

Unorthodox garments from Japan, although challenging to consumers and critics of the time, showed an extraordinary richness of texture, from unbleached, wrinkled felt to distressed or boiled textiles, dyeing in the style of *aizome* (a traditional indigo-dyed fabric) and subtle patterns woven in black on black. Eschewing existing materials, these fashion designers joined forces with Japanese textile designers and technologists to develop their own fabrics with which to create garments of striking originality. Silhouettes evolved organically from the inherent characteristics of the fabrics used.

The relationship and level of collaboration between these designers and the Japanese textile industry are unparalleled around the globe. Japan has over the centuries developed a sophisticated textile industry and, since World War II, has invested heavily in the regeneration of its manufacturing and industrial base. In order to compete with new fashions from the West, however, it was the synthetic-fibre industry that developed in leaps and bounds, rather than the traditional Japanese textile sector. The pioneering efforts of synthetics manufacturers, who inherited the dedication to high-quality innovation characteristic of traditional, organic-textile producers, spawned a new generation of technically advanced synthetic fibres, dyeing methods and weaving techniques. Japanese fashion designers have collaborated in the development of these materials, from the choice of thread at the very beginning of the manufacturing process to the completion of the garment.

Issey Miyake is a pioneer in his collaboration with the Japanese textile industry. From the very beginning of his career in the 1970s, the designer, along with his textile director Makiko Minagawa, has not only used traditional fabrics slowly being abandoned – for example, *oniyoryu* (a thick cotton crêpe) or *shijiraori* (a cloth from Awa usually woven by women using discarded pieces of cotton) – but also introduced modern technologies to develop new textiles. In the late 1980s and early 1990s Miyake developed and refined his revolutionary pleating technique, in which polyester is cut into the shape of a garment several times the desired final size and then heat-pressed to create permanent pleats. In 1999 Miyake launched the 'A-POC' concept – a truly innovative method of clothing manufacture integrating the weaving and sewing processes (see 'Flatness', pages 63, 80–83).

Innovation in the field of textiles is still very much in vogue with younger Japanese designers, most prominently in the work of Junya Watanabe. This self-styled 'techno-couturier' reconstructs clothing by creating new textiles that blend natural and synthetic fibres and applying revolutionary cutting techniques to them. For example, instead of forming and shaping through the traditional use of darts, he has developed his own tailoring technique using origami-like folds in fabric slashed at the body's joints. He also combines industrial and 'techno' materials with classic tailoring or evening wear to produce high-performance garments, often resulting in a catwalk spectacle: in his Spring/Summer 2000 show, models dressed in shifts and evening gowns made from his ultra-lightweight and waterproof fabrics were showered with water on the runway (see page 209).

Like Watanabe, Final Home designer Kosuke Tsumura utilizes the latest technical fabrics in his multi-purpose and resolutely urban designs. The Final Home wearer is, in transparent jacket or tent-like coat that he has padded himself, sheltered and secured against every unforeseen eventuality (see pages 106–107). 'When one loses his house, the thing that protects in the end is cloth', says Tsumura.[1]

Yohji Yamamoto continually reinvents the traditions of East and West through sophisticated yet simplified modernist expression. His appropriation of the shapes, techniques and fabrics of kimono for modern attire – most explicitly acknowledged in his Spring/Summer 1995 collection – pays homage to the high status of kimono and its enduring appeal, despite its disappearance as everyday dress. The latest generation of designers, in particular Hiroyuki Horihata and Makiko Sekiguchi of Matohu, continue to revive traditional kimono-making techniques but imbue their designs with a contemporary edge and an eye to the practicalities of modern urban living (see pages 57, 111). Other young designers have given a modern twist to such traditional Japanese fabrics as paper, which was historically used for *kamiko* – a type of kimono worn by priests. Tao Kurihara's Spring/Summer 2007 collection presented ultra-feminine paper wedding dresses and skirts worn with sporty silk-knit polo shirts (see pages 100–101). Hiroaki Ohya's 'Wizard of Jeanz' series of conceptual garments all start life as a closed book and unfold in the manner of giant origami or paper lanterns into a range of spectacular paper denim skirts, knit pieces and a concertina paper cape, skirt and dress (see page 105).

Recasting tradition has also taken the form of the deconstruction and, therefore, reconstruction of fashion conventions. Rei Kawakubo has relentlessly sought to confront the expected in fashion: 'I want to create something new', she once said. 'I want to suggest to people different aesthetics and values. I want to question their being.'[2] Kawakubo's collections have consistently achieved this ambition through a startling re-imagining of body, fabric and form. Her deconstruction of modes of Western tailoring routinely questions the necessary symmetry of a garment (be it hemline, waistline, shoulder or lapel), the 'correct' placement of a sleeve or seam or the assumed beauty of the idealized female form.

The ability of Japan's designers to demonstrate their unconventional creative talents owes much to both modern Japan's textile sector, underpinned as it is by a long and venerable textile culture, and an enduring commitment to finding new forms of expression. The results consistently fascinate and continue to push forward the boundaries of fashion.

1. Kosuke Tsumura, www.finalhome.com/en/2006/10/final_home.php (accessed 28 July 2010).
2. Quoted in an interview with Susannah Frankel, *Guardian Weekend Magazine*, 1 March 1997.

Junya Watanabe/Junya Watanabe Comme des Garçons
Autumn/Winter 2000–01
Adriana pour Watanabe, 2000
Photograph by Sarah Moon

Junya Watanabe/
Junya Watanabe Comme des Garçons
Autumn/Winter 2000–01
Off-white dress in nylon pile on nylon/
polyester ground; white polyester
organdie ruff collar

The sublime, ethereal chiffon ensembles from Junya Watanabe's 'Techno Couture' collection of Autumn/Winter 2000–01 are arguably his most romantic yet. The voluminous skirt shown opposite is made from a complex honeycomb-structured polyester that creates a delicate sculptural silhouette. The skirt packs completely flat and, when worn, expands to recover its three-dimensionality. It is teamed with a jacket made from nine layers of ultra-fine polyester organdie cut out using a heat-cutting technique. The somewhat inorganic palette of intense reds, yellows and azure blues characteristic of synthetic fibres tempered the whimsical delicacy of the 'Techno Couture' collection. Other pieces in the collection included the exaggerated ruff above, which surpassed anything conceived possible in the sixteenth and seventeenth centuries. Extending over the shoulders to encompass the torso, this collar, too, was made in polyester – the only fibre that could achieve the requisite stiffness to retain the garment's shape.

Junya Watanabe started his own label under the umbrella of Comme des Garçons in 1992, and seeks to create twenty-first-century couture that harnesses the Japanese textile industry's innovations in synthetic-fibre technology.

Junya Watanabe/Junya Watanabe Comme des Garçons
Autumn/Winter 2000–01
Red polyester organdie jacket; yellow polyester
organdie skirt

Jun Takahashi/Undercover
Spring/Summer 2007
Red polyester organdie halter-neck dress,
covered in red skull-shaped decorations

Koji Tatsuno
Autumn/Winter 1993–94
Golden brown nylon net dress
Photograph by Richard Burbridge
Published in *Frieze*, no. 7,
November–December 1993

In 1980 Koji Tatsuno moved to London,
where he taught himself fashion design,
taking on the challenge of producing unique
garments by utilizing innovative methods and
experimenting with rare craft techniques.
'I like to create in a spontaneous way', the
designer has said. 'The convention is that you
start from a flat fabric cut out on a surface but
that to me has nothing to do with the body.'[1]

Tatsuno first captured attention in 1983
when he co-launched the label Culture Shock.
From 1990 to 1994 he participated in the Paris
collections as Koji Tatsuno. While involved
with prêt-à-porter, he also presented art-
orientated garments, which he described as

'one-offs', made with extraordinary patterns and
such fabrics as dried seaweed and coils of rope.

This dress's voluminous flounces were
created by sewing layers of nylon net into spirals
and combining the small circles into larger units
of two. The unique, flamboyant structure is
typical of Tatsuno. This garment was later worn
by the main character in the film *The Pillow
Book* (1996), directed by Peter Greenaway.

1. Quoted in Roger Tredre, 'Prototypes from the
Perimeters', *The Independent*, 17 July 1993.

Rei Kawakubo/Comme des Garçons
Autumn/Winter 1990–91
White dress of non-woven fabric,
with ribbon around hem
Photograph by Niall McInerney

It is the soft, non-woven fabric used in this wedding dress that creates the full yet light form reminiscent of a Victorian-era crinoline dress. The handkerchief hemline of the skirt consists of three layered, square fabric pieces; the inclusion of a drawstring provides the possibility of transforming the hemline, adding further movement to the skirt. With its unusual cutting-edge fabric and form, this wedding dress has been given an ultra-modern treatment. However, Rei Kawakubo has not forgotten to maintain the neatness, prettiness and elegance required of this most special garment type, which is expected to be somewhat traditional.

Rei Kawakubo/Comme des Garçons
Autumn/Winter 1997–98
Beige bonded wool dress with golden foil
and cord stitching, on polyester organdie
dress with gold embroidery; red nylon/
polyester stretch short leggings
Photograph by Anthea Simms

A polyester organdie dress forms the
foundation of this garment. Another dress
in sculpted bonded wool is layered over the
organdie base to create a new deconstructed
'couture': the asymmetric wool panels do not
meet as convention would dictate, and the
central, transparent base layer reveals an
unexpected pair of short, sporty leggings.

The mass of the stiff bonded wool contrasts
with the elegant gold foil, cord stitching
and large floral pattern and with the
transparency of the base layer, demonstrating
Rei Kawakubo's extraordinary design vision
and her unique talent for combining
seemingly incompatible materials, textures
and forms.

Rei Kawakubo/Comme des Garçons
Autumn/Winter 1997–98
Photograph by Annie Leibovitz
Published in American *Vogue*, September 1997

Deconstruction:
Exposing the Invisible, Unhinging the Establishment

The term 'deconstruction' originated in the writings of French philosopher Jacques Derrida in the late 1960s. The philosophy aimed at unbuilding the constructs of a culture inherited from previous generations, and held language and its structure as key. Using free association, near-rhymes, puns and maddening digressions in an effort to decentralize established thinking, Derrida stood at the helm of a philosophical overhaul.

Designers and critics later took up the term 'deconstruction', and gave iteration to a pervasive mood in Western society set on debunking established modes of design. Where Derridean deconstruction challenged the non-visible form of meaning, such disciplines as architecture and fashion picked up on the 'construction' in 'deconstruction' as it applied to their own visible fields. In architecture, 'construction' refers to the precepts of building; in clothing, to a set of traditional rules for tailoring and fashion. The word can even be used in relation to music, where it implies the visible arrangement of harmonies. To 'deconstruct' in these disciplines is to dismantle the form. Dislodging the term from its philosophical origins, designers and artists established an aesthetic of fragmentation, disruption and displacement.

In fashion, it can be argued that the first manifestation of deconstruction began on the streets of London. Following the effeminate mods and leather-clad rockers, in the 1970s punk emerged as an aggressive counterculture. Punks' shredded black garb was a publication of outrage and antipathy to society. These anarchist libertarians established a significant 'tear down' and 'destroy' aesthetic, and the influential 'punk look' became associated with clothing that was worn unfinished, inside out and ravaged.

In the early 1980s Japanese designers Rei Kawakubo, Yohji Yamamoto and Issey Miyake seemed to incarnate a similar distress in relation to Western fashion. The look promoted ragged edges, irregular hemlines, crinkled fabrics and ill-fitting layers, and was termed 'Le Destroy' by the French. However, influenced by the minimalism of their own art and culture, these designers imbued their ripped, reversed and asymmetrical garments with a brutal sophistication. They pioneered what can legitimately be considered a fashion revolution, exposing the construction of garments on the catwalk stage.

A decade later a second wave of deconstruction began, led by the Belgian designers Martin Margiela, Ann Demeulemeester and Dries Van Noten. This 1990s brand of deconstruction went beyond clothing construction and was a provocation to consumer culture itself. As the status of fashion designers rose to that of celebrities, Margiela established a cult of impersonality, refusing to be identified or photographed. Evading the seasonal structure of the industry, he launched his collections sporadically in offbeat locations, further deconstructing the conventions of the industry.

Deconstruction was originally an attitude of the time rather than a defined movement or methodology, a 'field' that flourished in the West, and today has become part of a formalized global cultural vocabulary. The approach has spread over the past forty years through architecture, music and design, establishing novel principles of practice. The exterior of a building does not have to be on the outside; music does not have to fill the gaps between notes; and clothing does not have to fit the body. Starting something does not have to lead to finishing it, and what is usually invisible does not have to remain unseen.

Cher Potter

Rei Kawakubo/Comme des Garçons
Spring/Summer 1999
Photograph by Niall McInerney

mintdesigns
Autumn/Winter 2008–09
Printed shirtcoat of paper-like plain-weave polyester cloth; white and navy-blue wool patterned trousers
Photograph by Yoshitsugu Enomoto

The lightweight coat above and the dress pictured opposite are made from a polyester material ordinarily used to make sails for yachts, printed with the pages of a magazine in bright blue and transparent white. Envelopes used for the invitations to the

designers' catwalk show were shredded and recycled for use on the dress, adding volume to the skirt. With their distinctly pop sensibility, these pieces are characteristic of mintdesigns' predilection for fun printed and laser-cut motifs.

The label was formed in 2001 by Hokuto Katsui and Nao Yagi, who met while studying at Central Saint Martins College in London, and they debuted their designs at the Tokyo collections in 2003. Research and experimentation are the driving forces of their approach to design.

While working in close partnership with a small factory, the duo gained an understanding of the blurring and shearing that sometimes occur accidentally during the printing process – an insight they have subsequently incorporated into their print designs. They have also introduced such industrial fabrics as 'Smash', a thermoplastic unwoven fabric manufactured by the Asahi Kasei Fibers Corporation, with which the designers have collaborated in their drive to expand the possibilities of the Japanese textile industry.

mintdesigns
Autumn/Winter 2008–09
Polyester plain-weave dress with blue
magazine motif print and decoration
of envelope waste on skirt

Tao Kurihara/Tao Comme des Garçons
Spring/Summer 2007
White silk-knit short-sleeve polo shirt; white
kraft-paper skirt over white synthetic tulle
waistband; white cotton gloves

For Spring/Summer 2007, Tao Kurihara, who
launched her own label under Comme des
Garçons in 2005 (Tao Comme des Garçons),
presented an entirely white collection titled

'A Shirt and a Wedding'. Bringing to mind
the traditional Japanese craft of origami, the
paper streamers that form the skirt of this
piece, falling from a synthetic tulle concertina-
folded waistband, were painstakingly
constructed by folding, tying and threading
by hand. The delicate paper skirt, finished
with a series of sweet folded-paper bows and
ultra-feminine white gloves, is juxtaposed
with a sporty and masculine silk-knit polo

shirt. The ensemble traverses the boundary
between the everyday and the exceptional,
between masculine and feminine. In her review
of the collection, the revered journalist Suzy
Menkes said the designer 'gave a fresh take to
the essential idea that to make sense of clothes
for the modern woman, you have to start with
a male wardrobe'.[1]

1. Suzy Menkes, 'Robots and Androids: Balenciaga's
Future', *International Herald Tribune*, 3 October 2006.

Above: *Tao Kurihara/Tao Comme des Garçons*
Spring/Summer 2007
Photograph by Kirby Koh
Published in *i-D*, December 2007 – January 2008

Overleaf: *Rei Kawakubo/Comme des Garçons*
Spring/Summer 1998
Photographs by Jane McLeish Kelsey

Fashion editor Isabella Blow in Ohya
Spring/Summer 2000
Photograph by Mika Ninagawa

#01 ONEPIECE 1

#02 4 TANKTOP 2

THE WIZARD OF JEANZ
OHYA

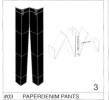

#03 PAPERDENIM PANTS 3

#04 PAPERDENIM SKIRT 4

#05 PAPERDENIM VEST 5

#06 PAPERDENIM ONEPIECE 6

#07 PAPERDENIM JACKET 7

#08 FAKEDENIM VEST 8

#09 FAKEDENIM SKIRT 9

#10 FAKEDENIM ONEPIECE 10

#11 FAKEDENIM V NECK ONEPIECE 11

#12 FAKEDENIM LONG ONEPIECE 12

#13 KNIT 13

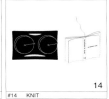

#14 KNIT 14

#15 KNIT 15

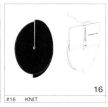

#16 KNIT 16

#17 FLOWER CAPE 17

#18 FLOWER SKIRT 18

#19 FLOWER ONEPIECE 19

#20 FLOWER SKIRT 20

#21 END ONEPIECE 21

Hiroaki Ohya/Ohya
'The Wizard of Jeanz', Spring/Summer 2000
Opposite: 'The Wizard of Jeanz' 17
Red polyester film cape with many layers,
which spreads out and expands like a beehive
and can be folded flat; attachment of indigo
denim as a cover
Above: Volumes 1–21; each with a case of
silver-coloured paper and black cotton, which
opens to form a garment. Hiroaki Ohya's
inspiration for the series' titles was the book
The Wizard of Oz by L. Frank Baum (1900)

HOW TO USE FINAL HOME

For use in emergencies, pockets
can be used to hold food and medicine;
cushions can be inserted into head
and shoulder pockets.
地震などの災害時に、非常食及び医薬品を詰め込み
頭部肩部にクッションを入れておきます。

For added comfort while watching
sporting events outdoors,
cushions can be inserted
into the hip pockets.
ヒップ部分にクッションを入れることで、
スポーツ観戦などに最適です。

FINAL
HOME

For added warmth outdoors, newspapers
can be inserted into the pockets.
都市及び自然の中でのサバイバルに、
新聞紙などを詰め込んで使用できます。

Final Home/Kosuke Tsumura
How to Use Final Home, 1994

Final Home/Kosuke Tsumura
1994
White nylon plain-weave coat

The Receptiveness of a Red Circle
on a White Background

The national flag of Japan is white with a red disk in the centre. We can say that the flag is a symbol that exemplifies the meaning of emptiness.

The red circle has no meaning. It is simply a red circle, and nothing beyond that. To give it a meaning such as nation, the Japanese emperor, or patriotism, is purely arbitrary. The fact that the red circle grabs our attention makes it an effective means of communicating and circulating whatever special meaning is used to fill it. Since it is initially empty, any meaning will do, whether it be invasion, destruction and imperialism, or patriotism and peace. Because I am of the postwar generation, I learned at school that the circle symbolizes a peaceful nation. I might create a big stir in the classroom if I mentioned this at a Chinese university, and I understand that there are people for whom such an interpretation would necessarily be painful. There was a fixed content in the so-called red circle for the countless soldiers who placed the flag on their foreheads and then went out and killed and died during World War II.

Yet the relationship between sign and meaning is arbitrary. You are basically free to interpret the circle as you wish; it could signify the sun in Shinto, for instance, or sincerity, or a pickled plum on a bed of rice. To those who were taught [that] the meaning of the circle was peace, it is seen as peace. I would like to reiterate, however, that the red circle by itself creates no meaning, only interpretation.

The symbolism of a fluttering white flag with a red disc in the centre functions independently, regardless of how people think of it. The Olympic banner, for example, generates a powerful centripetal force when it's raised, because it reflects the ideas and thoughts of people all over the world. This is the power of communication attached to the symbol.

Accordingly, the power of a symbol goes in tandem with its receptiveness. Because the simple and abstract quality of a red circle on a white background is so equivocal, it can be filled with various images. Its composition is one case where a figure signifies something only in relation to the background. In other words, the circle appears red when contrasted with white and its shape is circular in its relation to the rectangular background …

There aren't many symbols that possess such great receptivity. Perhaps the symbol of Christianity, the cross, is another good example in terms of its power to focus the mind.

Symbols' receptivity makes them attract attention and they can represent innumerable meanings. There is no right or wrong reading of a symbol. There may be different levels of receptiveness for a symbol in terms of its functionality; yet, since the symbol itself is empty to begin with, it can be neither evil nor good. If there is one aspect that might be seen as important, it is how its latent power is applied in a given situation. Therefore, even if our flag inevitably reflects a sad history, it can still hold every possible meaning if we place our will and hope in it. The Japanese flag fulfils its function silently while embracing the contradictory notions of sadness, disgrace, hope and peace.

Kenya Hara, White (*2010*)[1]

1. Excerpt from Kenya Hara, *White*, trans. Jooyeon Rhee, Baden, Switzerland (Lars Müller Publishers) 2010, pp. 48–50.

Rei Kawakubo/Comme des Garçons
Spring/Summer 2007
White triacetate/polyester tulle dress with
black nylon appliqué and red rayon flock
print with *hinomaru* (rising sun) motif
Photograph by Anthea Simms

Kenzo Takada/Kenzo
c. 1970
White acetate plain-weave dress with blue
printed bamboo and sparrow motifs

After studying at Bunka Fashion School in Tokyo in the early 1960s Kenzo Takada travelled to Europe, finally settling in Paris. He opened his first boutique, Jungle Jap, in 1970 and quickly gained a reputation for his bold use of fabric, print and colour. The first Jungle Jap collection featured on the cover of *Elle* magazine that year. This dress dates from the earliest Kenzo collections, and typifies his use of traditional motifs and simple silhouettes, which follow the straight, square cut of the kimono. In 1999 Kenzo retired from his fashion house, but the label continues under the creative direction of Antonio Marras and in 2010 celebrated its fortieth anniversary.

Matohu
Autumn/Winter 2009–10
Silk kimono-style coat with cotton/silk jersey sleeves, printed with brown and purple flower motif, gold stencil print and embroidery; purple cotton/silk jersey kimono-style dress, over beige cotton/silk jersey kimono-style dress; brown leather belt with fringe

This garment pays homage to the *Keicho kosode* – a style of kimono popular in the Keicho Period (1596–1615) in Japan. Common elements in the *Keicho kosode* style include the use of tie-dye techniques, vivid embroidery and gold-foil print. In this modern interpretation, the large printed leaf design contrasts with a base pattern of delicate plants and flowers, while embroidered embellishments add detail and texture and a foil print brings gold to the fore. Matohu, which in Japanese means 'to wear',

was established by designers Hiroyuki Horihata and Makiko Sekiguchi in 2005. Their passion for kimono culture started when the couple began collecting and wearing kimonos at weekends in Tokyo. 'For me, it was an inner revelation,' says Horihata, 'because when I walked in the street, I felt like a foreigner in Japan. Nobody wears kimonos now.'[1]

1. Quoted in Vanessa Lau, 'Turning Japanese', *W Magazine* (March 2010).

Yohji Yamamoto
Spring/Summer 1995
Catwalk presentation
Photograph by Niall McInerney

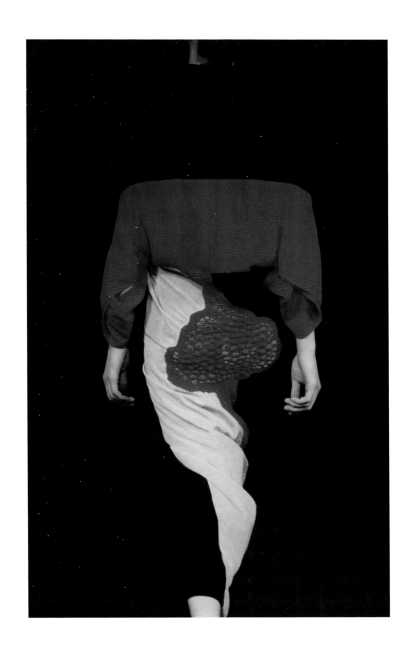

COOL JAPAN

'Forget the once vibrant and anarchic London streets. There is only one place where a passion for fashion still rules: Tokyo Is Now the World Capital of Street Style', declared fashion writer Suzy Menkes in 2000.[1] At that moment fashion audiences around the world and such internationally known designers as John Galliano were paying considerable attention to the phenomenon 'Cool Japan'.

Small groups of youths – or *zoku*, meaning 'tribe' – have always attracted considerable media attention in Japan and have defined the country's street style and subcultures for decades. The *taiyo-zoku* (sun tribe) of the 1950s was characterized by a spirit of reckless post-war abandon, akin to the 'rockers' and 'greasers' of 1950s America. The brightly clad, dancing *takenoko-zoku* (bamboo-shoot tribe) of the late 1970s and early 1980s carried the roots of Japanese street fashion. It was in the mid-1990s, however, that Tokyo's Shibuya and Harajuku districts gained a global reputation as the hot spot of youth fashion.

Japan's current youth fashions are characterized by a multitude of styles and influences: from the 'Lolita' look, cosplay (costume play) and manga to the take-up and reinterpretation of gothic, punk and American hip hop street styles. After the economic bubble of the 1980s burst and voracious youth appetite for global fashion brands began to wane, many young Tokyo-based designers started small fashion labels and opened independent shops, which were concentrated in the back streets of Harajuku – an area now known as Ura-Harajuku. This district had grown in popularity with students and young people, who congregated there on Sundays when Harajuku's main street was closed to traffic. This *hotoken* (literally 'pedestrian paradise') created a new kind of public sphere for Tokyo youth eager to meet their friends, chat and show off their unique outfits and styles.[2]

Jun Takahashi, once dubbed the 'guru of Ura-Harajuku', formed his label, Undercover, with a friend while still at fashion college. In 1993 he opened his first shop, the underground sensation Nowhere, in Harajuku. The space was divided between Takahashi and Tomoaki 'Nigo' Nagao, the DJ and designer who went on to create Japan's internationally renowned A Bathing Ape brand. Nowhere sold Takahashi's own line of hand-printed T-shirts alongside international street and sportswear brands, such as Nike and Adidas. The following year Undercover was formally established as a company and Takahashi brought the high-end, punk-influenced label to international attention when he began showing in the Paris collections in 2002 (see pages 126–28).

Like Takahashi, Fumito Ganryu takes influence from the street. The young designer launched his own label under the Comme des Garçons umbrella in 2007, with a women's collection that presented deconstructed hoodies, rabbit-print T-shirt dresses, and exaggerated collars made of calico dolls whose sweetness had dark undertones (see overleaf). His menswear mixes streetwear, workwear and skate-culture classics with simple, playful graphics and detailing.

The 'Lolita' look, derived from Vladimir Nabokov's mid-1950s novel of the same name, is typified by young girls' predilection for everything *kawaii* (cute) and a child-like sensibility expressed in Victorian and Rococo costume-inspired frills, petticoats, ribbons and bonnets. 'Lolita' fashion was worn by one of the main characters in the cult novel *Shimotsuma Monogatari* (2002) by author and fashion designer Novala Takemoto, known in Japan as 'Lolita's Bard'. The novel was adapted into a comic book and film (directed by Tetsuya Nakashima and released in 2004), and the Lolita look became widely known, first throughout Japan and then internationally when the film was released in the West under the title *Kamikaze Girls*.

Fumito Ganryu/Comme des Garçons
Spring/Summer 2008
Ivory polyester knit dress with
thirty-three dolls made of white cotton

Japanese gothic Lolita style, or 'Goth-Loli', blends the cute and feminine frills and ribbons of the Lolita look with the all-black style of Western goth subculture. Goth-Loli looks often feature frilly shirts worn with *paniers* or crinolines under knee-length pinafores and dresses. The look is completed with such accessories as black bows, crosses and platform Mary-Jane shoes. Tao Kurihara's debut collection in 2005 of knitted lingerie epitomized the nostalgic girlishness of the Lolita look (see pages 118–19). In her Autumn/Winter 2009–10 collection, darker overtones of the Goth-Loli style were evident, albeit fused with traditional European folk dress and Frida Kahlo-esque styling (see pages 138–41). As fashion curator Valerie Steele points out: 'The lines between sub-cultural style and high fashion have become increasingly blurred and not through any simple process of imitation.'[3]

It is no coincidence that Japanese street style – defined by artificiality exaggeration, and a girlish decorativeness – overlaps with images of heroines in *shōjo* manga (manga for girls, the personification of a narrative-driven girly taste): the ideal visual image replicated on the street is, undoubtedly, born of an aesthetic sensibility developed through influential manga and anime media. Such labels as Ohya have eschewed the visual overload common in Tokyo street fashion in favour of a simpler, more iconic use of such manga characters as Hello Kitty and Astro Boy (see page 122).

Kawaii is the catch-all term used internationally to describe this dominant trend in Japanese street fashion. *Kawaii* originally referred to something young or immature or something that, because of its small size, for example, makes one want to treat it with care; something cute. In recent years it has become a more specific adjective used by young women to describe a certain 'cool' sensibility. When the eponymous exhibition of the work of Japanese artist Takashi Murakami was held at the Fondation Cartier pour l'art contemporain in Paris in 2002, Murakami curated a concurrent exhibition of works titled *Kawaii! Vacances d'été* representing Japanese subcultures. In the autumn of the same year, high-end brand Louis Vuitton produced a range of designs featuring Murakami's manga and epitomizing the *kawaii* sensibility, catapulting the concept to an international high-fashion market.

However, in contrast to other street styles, or to such Western subcultures as punk and hip hop, Tokyo street style does not have a clear social message. Instead, it is characteristic of a strong desire for personal transformation through fashion and dress. Most significantly, young Japanese pursue the joy and fun of 'dressing up', mixing the real and virtual – as Lolita, Goth-Loli or manga characters – for pure individualistic and idiosyncratic self-expression.

1. Suzy Menkes, 'Tokyo Is Now the World Capital of Street Style: In the City and on the Catwalk, Japan Cultivates its Roots', *International Herald Tribune*, 14 November 2000.
2. Yuniya Kawamura, 'Placing Tokyo on the Fashion Map', in *Fashion's World Cities*, ed. Christopher Breward and David Gilbert, Oxford (Berg) 2006, p. 63.
3. Valerie Steele and Jennifer Park, *Gothic: Dark Glamour*, New Haven, Conn., and London (Yale University Press) 2008, p. 60.

Tao Kurihara/Tao Comme des Garçons
Autumn/Winter 2005–06
Ivory wool knit bodice with lacing;
cable-knit shorts

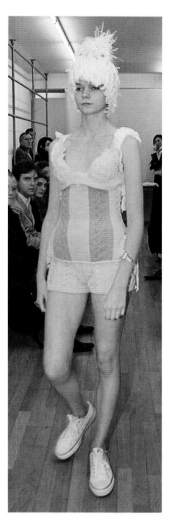

For her Paris debut for Tao Comme des Garçons in 2005, Tao Kurihara turned such classic undergarments as the camisole and brassiere into ultra-feminine knitted outerwear. From the forms of the bodices to the lace and ribbon decorative elements, the collection was based on a careful study of undergarments of the past, which were typically made from knitted wool. Tao's collections are often inspired by a single familiar item: a shirt, for example, or a handkerchief. The designer then transforms the seemingly everyday into an extraordinary collection of exquisitely detailed, cool yet feminine garments, desired by critics and consumers alike.

The coquettish woollen bodice opposite, decorated with an abundance of natural and beige woollen corsages and complete with matching cable-knit shorts, can be perfectly described as *kawaii* (cute). At the collection show, however, girlish cuteness was tempered with tomboy styling and accessories: some of the models wore the bodices over classic white T-shirts with black gym-style shorts and dazzlingly white Converse pumps.

Tao Kurihara/Tao Comme des Garçons
Autumn/Winter 2005–06
Collection presentation

Junya Watanabe/Junya Watanabe Comme des Garçons
Spring/Summer 2001
Five-layered dress of white transparent polyester
printed with cakes and tarts; imitation pearls at collar

Astro Boy: The Greatest Robot in the World
Cover illustration, Kappa Comics, 1965

Astro Boy's legendary creator, Osamu Tezuka, was a leading figure in Japan's post-war comics and TV boom, embedding manga and anime in the national consciousness. Tezuka came to fame as a teenager in 1946 with a number of groundbreaking comics, and he was a major celebrity by the time the Astro Boy manga appeared in 1951. In 1963 the animated Astro Boy joined the comics, live-action TV shows and radio plays carrying Tezuka characters into every Japanese home.

Tezuka was the first Japanese creator to set up a licensing department on the Disney model, and other companies soon followed his lead. Their influence pervades Japan's media. Anyone who watches TV, uses public transport or visits the supermarket cannot help but absorb the anime and manga aesthetic: character images adorn merchandise of all kinds, from food packaging to subway posters to dinnerware.

The digital marketplace boosted the worldwide popularity of Japanese comics and animation. Such cute twentieth-century playmates as Astro Boy, Hello Kitty and Hayao Miyazaki's anime heroines have become global media icons, uniting low and high art, playground and gallery. They are reinterpreted for twenty-first-century Japan by such fashion designers as Hiroaki Ohya, such illustrators as Lily Franky, or artists Takashi Murakami and Chiho Aoshima.

Fans pay homage to anime, manga and other fictions through cosplay (costume play), dressing as the characters they love. In common with 'Lolita' or punk stylers, cosplayers create alternative personas for self-expression, or just for fun. Chain stores, such as Animate and Gamers, each with over thirty outlets across Japan, offer cosplay items from TV shows and games, but store-bought costumes are frowned on by purists. They prefer to express their commitment to cosplay by crafting their own costumes and looks, coming closer to a couture aesthetic than to 'fancy dress'.

In Japanese cities – Kyoto, Osaka or World Cosplay Summit venue Nagoya – cosplayers are clearly visible. Some wear their chosen look in the street, others at clubs and conventions. At Tokyo's twice-yearly comic market Comiket, thousands of cosplayers display their skills to over half a million attendees. In re-creating a character, they remake aspects of themselves. For most, however, playing with identities is a transient phase, a game that is given up on leaving college or marrying. Although dressing up in traditional costume for festivals is accepted, it is rare for settled adults to cosplay.

Japanese street styles now appear worldwide, aided particularly by the international dissemination of such magazines as Fruits, and cosplay has ridden the coat-tails of anime and manga across international boundaries. Outside Japan, cosplayers are invisible on the streets unless there is a convention or event in the area, but there is an active forum-led community, with top-ranked international cosplayers travelling to Japan for Comiket and the World Cosplay Summit.

Popular new titles attract most cosplayers, but classic characters and shows keep reappearing. At Comiket 77 in December 2009, a devoted fan of 1986 anime Saint Seiya posed in a full bodysuit of winged, gold-plated armour. Because international film release schedules vary, Japanese cosplayers wear different characters from those in Britain, France or the USA. They love heroic teams in the Power Rangers mould and cute game characters. Catgirls are perennial favourites. Elaborate military uniforms, winged beasts and aliens offer a technical challenge.

Anime, manga and game cosplay strives to reproduce the look and persona of a character perfectly. This may seem to have little in common with the street tribes and stylers who create their own looks, but they are all informed by the ideal that drives Japanese fashion: the search for and expression of identity through the medium of clothing.

Helen McCarthy

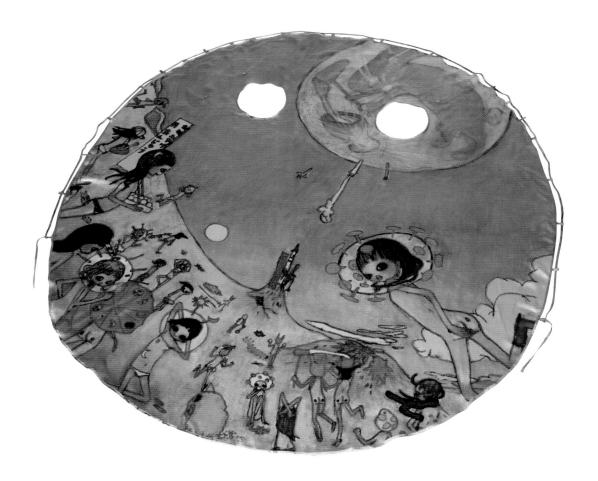

Naoki Takizawa for Issey Miyake
Spring/Summer 2004
Silk charmeuse circle-cut dress printed
with the work of artist Aya Takano; nylon
T-shirt and leggings

Naoki Takizawa was design director for Issey
Miyake from Spring/Summer 2000 until
Spring/Summer 2007. Since 1999 Takizawa
has collaborated with Japanese artist Takashi

Murakami and his artists' collective, KaiKai
Kiki, founded in 2001, a group famous for
being the first to incorporate manga elements
into its work.

This outfit is from the 'Journey to the
Moon' collection, produced in collaboration
with Japanese artist Aya Takano, another
member of KaiKai Kiki. Famous for her
super-flat drawing style and large-eyed
heroines, Takano is influenced by Japanese

mythology, manga and science fiction.
She created two images for the collection,
and this print, *The Moon from Earth*,
features sweet and child-like beings drawn
in the artist's typically innocent style,
faintly reminiscent of American sci-fi
'B movies'. In the moon itself, a rabbit is
seen pounding *mochi* (steamed rice) into
rice cakes, a motif that refers to Japanese
oral traditions.

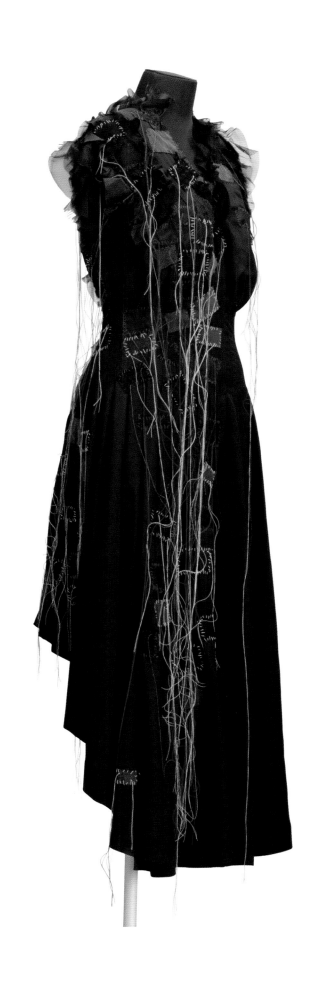

Jun Takahashi/Undercover
Spring/Summer 2003
Opposite: Black synthetic crêpe dress with
uneven hemline, appliqué, stitching and
strings hanging down
Above: 'Scab' collection catwalk presentation

Jun Takahashi began his career in Tokyo
as a standard-bearer for street fashion.
The dress opposite is from his first Paris
show, 'Scab', which was presented in 2002
and was motivated by the politics of the

time. The collection also called to mind
early punk and deconstructivist aesthetics.
The 'Scab' finale saw a procession of
models clad in vividly coloured, delicately
embellished burkas (above). 'I wanted to
mix a lot of cultural and ethnic stuff like
kilts and Afghan dresses to make humans
equal for once,' said the designer. 'I made
an anti-war collection.'[1]

On this ordinary-looking dress, small
pieces of linen and silk have been individually
but roughly hand-sewn to resemble 'scabs'.

From these flow countless coloured threads,
some in blood red, creating a somewhat
grotesque yet striking aesthetic. These
elements give the garment the feeling of
well-worn and frayed clothes, an aesthetic
the designer accentuates through his reverent
use of intricate handiwork. In contrast to
the output of modern mass production,
Takahashi's garments are beautifully crafted
and imbued with meaning.

1. Quoted in Nicole Fall, 'Light and Magic', *i-D*,
March 2003, p. 196.

Jun Takahashi/Undercover
Spring/Summer 2006
Beige wool tricot vest with white cotton
fringe; white cotton T-shirt and skirt
Photograph by Dan Lecca

STREET STYLE

THE HISTORY OF POST-WAR JAPANESE STREET STYLE IS PEPPERED WITH *ZOKU* (TRIBES): GROUPS OF SARTORIALLY ADVENTUROUS YOUTH WITH A PARTICULAR LOOK OR MUSIC TASTE AND A VERY PUBLIC PRESENCE. THESE *ZOKU* HAVE, LIKE THE HEADS OF THE MYTHICAL HYDRA, CONTINUALLY MULTIPLIED AND DIVIDED INTO SUBCATEGORIES, MAKING JAPAN ONE OF THE MOST STYLISTICALLY DIVERSE COUNTRIES IN THE WORLD AND PROVIDING A RICH SUBSTRATE ON WHICH HIGH FASHION THRIVES. IN THE TYPICAL 'TRICKLE-DOWN' THEORY, FASHIONS SEEN ON THE STREET FOLLOW THOSE ON THE CATWALK, BUT NOW THE FLOW OF INSPIRATION AND TRENDS BETWEEN EAST AND WEST, STREET AND CATWALK IS MULTIDIRECTIONAL.

MAGAZINES HAVE FACILITATED THE GLOBAL FLOW OF IMAGES AND ARE CONSUMED VORACIOUSLY IN JAPAN. THE RANGE ON THE SHELVES TESTIFIES TO THE VARIOUS DISTINCT NICHES OF 'TRIBAL' LOOKS TO BE FOUND TODAY. PHOTOGRAPHER AND PUBLISHER SHOICHI AOKI HAS BEEN INSTRUMENTAL IN THIS ENTERPRISE, FIRST BRINGING IMAGES FROM PARIS, LONDON AND OTHER FASHION CAPITALS TO JAPAN THROUGH THE MAGAZINE *STREET*, THEN DOCUMENTING THE BURGEONING STREET-FASHION SCENES IN TOKYO AND OSAKA WITH THE MAGAZINES *FRUITS* AND, LATTERLY, *TUNES*.

IN SOME WAYS, THOUGH, 'STREET FASHION' IS A MISLEADING TERM: THESE CREATIVE LOOKS DO NOT JUST WELL UP FROM THE PAVING STONES BUT ARE SEEDED AND CULTIVATED IN SPECIFIC LOCATIONS. FOR THE MODE KEI (FASHION STYLE) YOUTH OF URA-HARAJUKU – WHO MATCH THE HIGH FASHION OF SUCH DESIGNERS AS JEREMY SCOTT, BERNHARD WILHELM, UNDERCOVER AND COMME DES GARÇONS WITH SECOND-HAND, VINTAGE AND REMADE CLOTHES – FASHION SCHOOLS, SELECT SHOPS AND CLUB EVENTS ARE IMPORTANT BREEDING GROUNDS. FOR 'LOLITAS', MUCH OF THEIR SARTORIAL DISPLAY AND EXCHANGE HAPPENS AT SHOPS, TOO, BUT ALSO AT VISUAL KEI (AN EXTREME STYLE ASSOCIATED WITH JAPANESE ROCK BANDS) ROCK CONCERTS. MANY *GYARU* (GALS) WITH THEIR SASSY FAST FASHION USE FAST-FOOD RESTAURANTS AS THEIR SOCIAL BASES.

WHILE THERE IS A RICH MISCELLANY OF STYLES TODAY IN TOKYO, *KAWAII* ('CUTE') HAS BEEN AN ENDURING AESTHETIC IN THE MATERIAL CULTURE OF EVERYDAY JAPAN. HELLO KITTY IS THE STEREOTYPICAL *KAWAII* ICON. HER IMAGE HAS HAD A NEW SPIN PUT ON IT IN RECENT YEARS THROUGH COLLABORATIONS WITH EVERYTHING FROM AVANT-GARDE FASHION LABELS TO LOLITA AND PUNK BRANDS. *KAWAII* HAS EXPANDED FROM SYMBOLIZING WHAT SHARON KINSELLA, AN EXPERT ON JAPANESE VISUAL CULTURE, SEES AS A PASSIVE RESISTANCE TO ADULTHOOD, ENTERING INSTEAD THE REALM OF THE SUBVERSIVE.[1] THIS EMPOWERMENT OF CUTE CAN BE SEEN IN TAO KURIHARA'S KNITTED UNDERWEAR AS OUTERWEAR COLLECTION, MIXING HOMELY INNOCENCE WITH SEDUCTION IN A HIGH-FASHION CONTEXT (SEE PAGES 118–19). CUTE HAS BECOME DARKER, TOO: MANY POPULAR SOFT-TOY CHARACTERS ARE NOW SCARRED AND DRIP WITH BLOOD. 'GOTH-LOLI', WITH ITS VICTORIAN RUFFLES AND GOTH ICONOGRAPHY, IS PERHAPS THE ARCHETYPAL FUSION OF CUTE WITH DOOM AND GLOOM.

'LOLITA' STYLES APPEAR TO SEXUALIZE THEIR WEARERS, BUT TALK TO THE 'LOLITAS' AND IT BECOMES CLEAR THAT THEY ARE DRESSING FOR THEMSELVES AND NOT THE OPPOSITE SEX, FEELING PRETTIER IN THE CLOTHES. THE 'LOLITA' STYLE IS NOT TO BE MISTAKEN FOR THE EROTICIZED 'MAID' LOOK, WHICH IS VERY CLOSE AESTHETICALLY (SHORT PUFF SKIRTS, PINAFORES, FRILLS). THIS KIND OF SUBTLE DISTINCTIONS IS RIFE IN THE WORLD OF TOKYO YOUTH FASHION, MEANING THAT STYLES WITH ENTIRELY DIFFERENT SOCIAL ARTICULATIONS ARE OFTEN LUMPED TOGETHER BY ONLOOKERS.

TOKYO'S SPECTACULAR YOUTH STYLES VARY ESPECIALLY IN REGARD TO WHETHER THEY ARE WORN AS COSTUME OR FASHION. THE MANGA INSPIRATION USED BY HIROAKI OHYA AND NAOKI TAKIZAWA FOR ISSEY MIYAKE, FOR EXAMPLE, IS FAR REMOVED FROM THE COSTUMES IN WHICH HARD-CORE MANGA FANS COSPLAY THEIR FAVOURITE CHARACTERS. LOOKS THAT, LIKE PUNK, WE TYPICALLY ASSOCIATE WITH POLITICALLY SUBVERSIVE IDEOLOGIES AND NON-MAINSTREAM LIFESTYLES ARE OFTEN WORN MORE AS COSTUME IN JAPAN. FURTHERMORE, WEARING A STYLE ONLY SOME OF THE TIME, AS IS THE CASE WITH THE MANY 'LOLITAS' WHO DRESS UP AT WEEKENDS OR FOR GIGS, IS NOT NECESSARILY VIEWED AS INAUTHENTIC. ON THE OTHER HAND, FOR THE MODE KEI YOUTH IN HARAJUKU, THEIR STYLE SHOULD BE PERSONAL AND PERMANENT.

JAPAN IS OFTEN REGARDED AS A LAND OF CONFORMISTS WHO WILL DAMPEN THEIR INDIVIDUALITY IN ORDER TO BE LIKE OTHERS IN THE GROUP. HOWEVER, THE CURRENT GENERATION OF JAPANESE YOUTH TENDS TO OPERATE ON THE OPPOSITE IDEOLOGY, *JIBUN RASHII* (BEING TRUE TO ONESELF), WHETHER THROUGH CHOICE OF CAREER, CAR OR FASHION. THIS HAS LED SOME TO MOVE AWAY FROM SPECTACULAR STYLES TO ORGANIC, NATURAL, SIMPLE LOOKS, AS IN THE RECENT MORI (FOREST) GIRL STYLE, BUT THE RICH DIVERSITY OF TOKYO CULTURE CONTINUES TO THROW UP INSPIRING STREET AND CATWALK FASHIONS.

PHILOMENA KEET

1. Sharon Kinsella, 'Cuties in Japan',
Women, Media and Consumption in Japan,
ed. Lise Skov and Brian Moeran, Richmond
(Curzon Press) 1995.

Two teenagers in Tokyo wearing Pink Lolita
and Elegant Gothic Aristocrat looks.
Photograph by Yuri Manabe

Natsuki and Amiri relax in full
decora kei (decorative style) on
Tokyo's Jingubashi bridge.
Photograph by Yuri Manabe

Mine is cosplaying as Princess Lacus
Clyne from her favourite TV anime,
Gundam Seed.
Photograph by Yuri Manabe

Yushi, left, and Hidekazu, right,
are dressed in the hip hop style.
Photograph by Yuri Manabe

Yulia, left, is a Tokyo DJ; Bizarru runs
the shop Candy in Shinjuku ni-chome,
the city's gay district.
Photograph by Yuri Manabe

Ao, left, dressed like the lead singer of the
Visual-kei rock band Dir-en-Grey; Gyowaro,
right, dressed as herself.
Photograph by Yuri Manabe

Jun Takahashi/Undercover
Spring/Summer 2003
Off-white cotton jacket with epaulettes,
appliqué and stitching on the front, and
chiffon at back; off-white cotton trousers,
with cotton tapes, appliqué and stitching;
white leather bracelet with bells

Tao Kurihara/Tao Comme des Garçons
Autumn/Winter 2009–10
Black polyester tulle overshirt with flower embroidery; printed white polyester chiffon blouse; red polyester plain-weave overskirt with ribbon; red wool and mohair twill skirt with tulle

In an interview with Japanese magazine *High Fashion* in 2009, Tao Kurihara revealed her starting point when designing a collection: 'I start with a new technique … something which manipulates fabric in a way that I've never done before, which begs me to explore what kind of clothing I can create from it.' For the 'Decoration Accident' collection (above), Tao challenged herself to express new forms of ornamentation by 'taking the base fabric and twisting and tying it up with ribbons and making the design become one big decoration'.[1]

The frothy silhouettes of the 'Decoration Accident' baby-doll dresses, skirts, cross-stitched pantaloons and quilted jackets have an abundant volume created by using a bullion smocking technique, which joins several gathers in a single complex knotted stitch. The collection blends folkloric nostalgia with inspiration from Eastern Europe and Mexico, producing an unexpected cuteness. It is as if a dress designed for a doll seen in a dream has been brought to life.

1. Quoted in Maya Nago, 'Freedom, a Rigorous Battle and a Pure Wish', *High Fashion* (October 2009).

Scrapbook by fashion observer/illustrator
Lele Acquarone published in Italian *Vogue*,
September 2009

Tao Kurihara/Tao Comme des Garçons
Autumn/Winter 2009–10
Photograph by Ben Hassett
Styling by Erika Kurihara
Published in *i-D*, Fall 2009

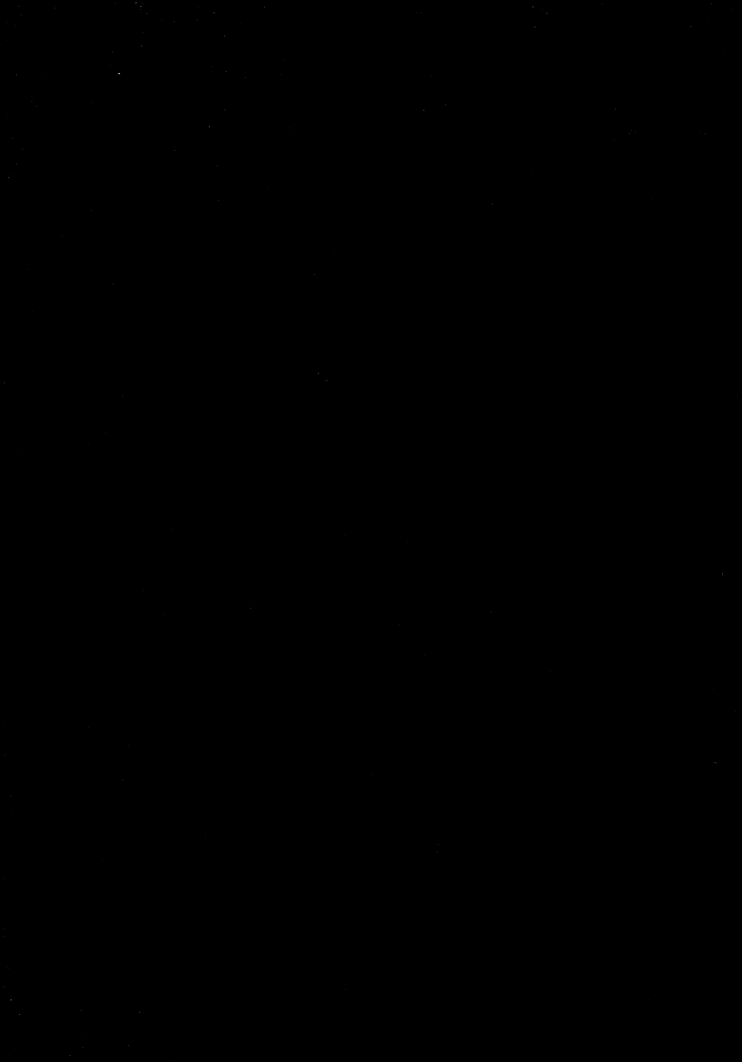

ISSEY MIYAKE

It is impossible to resist attributing Issey Miyake's gentle spirit at least in part to the fact that he was born in Hiroshima. On 6 August 1945 he was seven years old and cycling to school when the Americans dropped the atom bomb. Miyake lost most of his family, and his mother was severely burned, although she carried on working as a schoolteacher for four years before she died.

When he was ten, Miyake himself developed bone-marrow disease, the effects of which he suffers to this day. Reluctant to talk about it, Miyake prefers to dwell on happier aspects of his childhood: a beautiful bridge in his home town, which he cites as his first consciousness of design; stopping his bicycle to press his nose up against shop windows and admire the mannequins. 'They changed every month, those windows. I saw myself in them. I was fascinated.'[1] Still, backstage at his Autumn/Winter 1995–96 show in Paris, more than a hundred assistants wore white T-shirts printed with a dove of peace to commemorate the fiftieth anniversary of the bombing of Hiroshima. The critic Mark Holborn has written: 'Miyake's creativity exists not in detachment from the shadows of Japanese history, but in an inescapable response to such experience. His career corresponds exactly to the recovery of the nation, and it is there in Japan, after both Paris and America, that his own sense of definition is established.'[2]

At the age of twenty-six, Miyake left Tama Art University in Tokyo with a degree in graphic design. He arrived in Paris in 1965, enrolled with the École de la Chambre syndicale de la couture parisienne and worked first with Guy Laroche, then for Givenchy, before moving to New York, where he was employed by Geoffrey Beene. 'I was faced with the heavy tradition that was French high society,' the designer has said of his first experience in the French fashion capital, 'and felt I couldn't go through with it. I thought, "I am Japanese!" I used to escape to London once a month to relax. That was my place. There was the King's Road, the fantastic Biba store, there were musicals – I remember *Oliver!* Shepherd's pie.'

It was to Tokyo, however, and to a country undergoing enormous cultural and economic change, that Miyake returned to set up his design studio in 1970. This was the year of the Osaka Expo, and a time when, despite, or perhaps because of, the deprivation experienced by the generation that grew up during the war or early occupation, creativity was burgeoning. 'The prevalent Americanisation of the occupation was replaced by the possibility of an independent Japanese culture which accommodated both native and Western traditions with a new modernity', according to Holborn. Japan was 'a nation at the height of its reconstruction under the gaze of symbols of its past'.[3]

Although the Issey Miyake label is still shown in Paris and is now an international brand, its namesake and the company Miyake founded still reside in Tokyo. While his early work focused on *sashiko* – the quilted cotton worn by Japanese peasants – and he has continually reinterpreted certain aspects of traditional Japanese garments, including the kimono and the fisherman's tunic, Miyake nevertheless resents being pigeonholed as a Japanese designer. His clothes, he has always said, are indebted to Japanese tradition, just as they are to American, French and even English heritage: 'I had to be free of the Occidental way, of Occidental ideas, but there are still a lot of things to learn from them. It is very important to keep tradition.'

Issey Miyake
Folded garment from the '132 5' collection,
2010 (see page 148)
Photograph by Hiroshi Iwasaki/Stash

At least some of Miyake's designs are extreme to the point where they have seemed more at home in a gallery setting or indeed flattened and captured as objects by the lens of Irving Penn. Bodices constructed of bamboo and rattan, waxed-paper jackets and hats, and Crayola-coloured neoprene all-in-ones are just three examples. His is a comparatively democratic approach, nonetheless. In 1988, in a testimony to a career-long fascination with fabric research, Miyake first started working with pleats, and with the subsequent launch of 'Pleats Please' in 1993 – a more accessibly priced and practical line of clothing – he drove that mindset home.

'My first dream,' Miyake has since argued, 'and why I first decided to open my studio, was that I thought: "If I could one day make clothes like T-shirts and jeans, I would be very excited." But … I was always doing such heavy things, far away from the people. And then I was thinking, you know, "Are you stupid? Don't you remember why you started designing in the first place?" And then I thought, "Okay, Pleats Please." So I started to think how to make it, how to wash it, how to coordinate it, even how to pack it. And I worked on how to keep the price down.'

The 'Pleats Please' line is indeed machine washable and, when packed, the pieces roll up into pretty pleated coils, from which they emerge, quite miraculously, unscathed. Whether horizontal or vertical, the pleats give the clothes elasticity and make them extremely easy to wear: 'To me, design must get into real life. Otherwise, it's just couture, it's just extravaganza.'

In 1999, in collaboration with textile engineer Dai Fujiwara, Miyake went on to add 'A-POC' (from 'A Piece of Cloth' and a play on the word 'epoch') to his repertoire. An entire outfit is cut out of a single piece of fabric by the consumer, who is offered traced guidelines by the designer but is actively encouraged to adapt to her own taste (see pages 63, 80–83).

Issey Miyake retired in the late 1990s and the company's then design director Naoki Takizawa was named designer of the main line. In 2007 Fujiwara took over both roles, and he has since continued to uphold not only the Miyake aesthetic but also the pioneering long-term research into both fabric and garment design that the designer always valued so highly.

1. Issey Miyake, quoted in Susannah Frankel, 'Between the Pleats', *Guardian Weekend Magazine*, 19 July 1997. This is the source for all Issey Miyake quotations in this section, unless otherwise indicated.
2. Mark Holborn, *Issey Miyake*, Cologne (Taschen) 1995.
3. *Ibid.*

132 5
'A piece of flat material becomes a three-dimensional structure (3D). The structure, in turn, becomes a two-dimensional shape with the addition of straight folding lines (2D). When the new shape is put on the human body, it becomes clothing (5D). The project name is derived from this process

of transformation. It was born from the Miyake Design Studio's continuous search for new ways by which to industrialize recycling, based upon experience with polyester fibre. New PET (polyethylene terephthalate) material is born from the old, recycling both limited resources and energy and returning

CO_2 to the earth. This is the starting point for the future of making things.'
Miyake Design Studio, 2010[1]

1. Statement from Miyake Design Studio for *Future Beauty: 30 Years of Japanese Fashion* book, July 2010.

Issey Miyake
'132 5' collection, 2010
Polyester top and skirt pressed with metal
foil (opposite), folded into 'Y' shapes
Photographs by Hiroshi Iwasaki/Stash

Issey Miyake
'132 5' collection, 2010
Polyester top and skirt pressed with metal
foil (opposite), folded into octagons
Photographs by Hiroshi Iwasaki/Stash

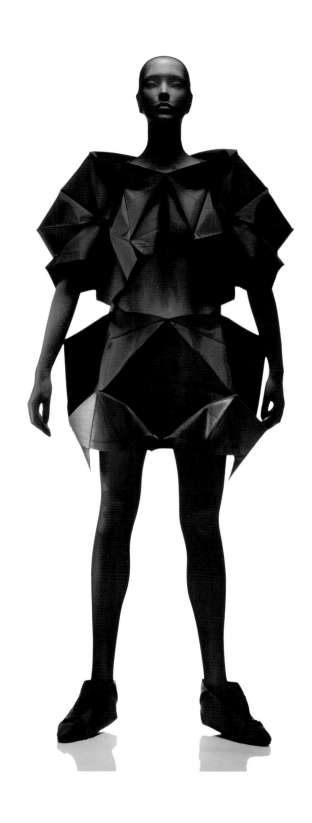

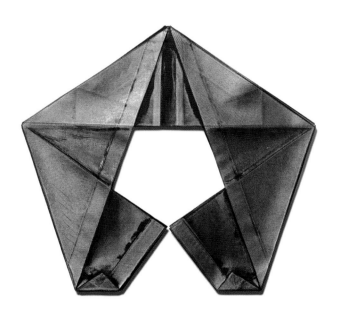

Issey Miyake
'1 3 2 5' collection, 2 0 1 0
Polyester top and skirt pressed with metal
foil (opposite), folded into polygons
Photographs by Hiroshi Iwasaki/Stash

Issey Miyake
'132 5' collection, 2010
Polyester top and skirt pressed with metal
foil (opposite), folded into octagons
Photographs by Hiroshi Iwasaki/Stash

Issey Miyake
'1 3 2 5' collection, 2010
Polyester dress pressed with metal foil
(opposite), folded into polygons
Photographs by Hiroshi Iwasaki/Stash

Issey Miyake
'1 3 2 5' collection, 2 0 1 0
Polyester dress pressed with metal foil
(opposite), folded into polygons
Photographs by Hiroshi Iwasaki/Stash

REI KAWAKUBO

Rei Kawakubo is the world's most influential living fashion designer. Oversized garments that envelop the female form rather than, in the bourgeois tradition, exposing it, boiled knitwear and, most significantly, the establishment of black as fashion's default (non-)colour of choice are all part of her legacy and have long since become key elements of the contemporary fashion lexicon.

Born in Tokyo in 1942, the daughter of a senior faculty member at Keio University, Kawakubo started school while Japan was still occupied by the US army. 'By the time she graduated,' wrote Deyan Sudjic in his 1990 monograph on her label, Comme des Garçons, 'the country had decisively emerged from the ranks of the developing world. The ferment of those years provided unique opportunities for the members of a generation that was ready to make the most of them. They enjoyed the fruits of an economic success story which enabled Japan to look at the outside world in more objective terms, to make its own creative contribution and in the process to assert its own identity as a mature modern state.'[1]

After studying fine art and literature, Kawakubo worked as a stylist in the advertising department of a major chemical manufacturer. Discovering an affinity with the photographers and art directors with whom she collaborated on outside projects, she went freelance, and, when she could not find the clothes she wanted in order to do her job in an interesting way, she turned to designing them herself. Remarkably, she had no formal fashion training. 'I wanted to have some kind of job to earn money,' she has said, 'because at that time, having money meant being free. I never dreamt of being a fashion designer like other people. When I was young, it was just a way of earning a living by doing something I found I could do.'[2]

Kawakubo claims that she named her company Comme des Garçons ('like boys') simply because she liked the way it sounds, insisting that there is no underlying political meaning, although it may be tempting to believe otherwise. In 1981, with the label well established in Japan, the designer presented a small collection in Paris. It was not, however, until the Paris show for Spring/Summer 1983 that Comme des Garçons caused a scandal.

The collection was called 'Destroy', and the presentation – models exiting in groups to cold, flashing lights – was as unconventional as the clothes. As for the latter, skirts had jacket sleeves hanging from the front of them; trousers had sweater cuffs at the ankles; oversized coats for women buttoned from left to right, *comme des garçons*; shoes were flat, rustic even, at a time when high heels and high fashion went hand in hand; even the models' lipstick was displaced, painted to one side of their mouths on their cheeks. With a fashion establishment that boasted, at one end of the spectrum, the 'jolies madames' of Chanel, Dior and Yves Saint Laurent, and, at the other, more radical and clearly status-driven 1980s uber-designers, such as Frenchmen Thierry Mugler and Claude Montana and Italians Gianni Versace and Giorgio Armani, Kawakubo's vision was simply too extreme a contrast to digest. It is the stuff of fashion folklore that more than a few critics left the space in tears.

Rei Kawakubo/Comme des Garçons
Spring/Summer 1997
Photograph by Nick Knight
(See page 170)

Some thirty years on, Kawakubo has dedicated her life to the creation of ever more inspirational collections that continue to challenge our preconceptions of how women – and indeed men – like to dress. Over that period, statements have been as diverse as the infamous 'Body Meets Dress, Dress Meets Body' collection (Spring/Summer 1997) – the designer's personal favourite, featuring padding that was far from conventionally flattering at shoulders and hips (see pages 163–69); 'Beyond Taboo' (Autumn/Winter 2001–02), which reworked the clichés of erotica to thoroughly subversive effect; and 'Witch' (Autumn/Winter 2004–05), which revisited the strength of black clothing, taking in everything from Victorian mourning dress to Kawakubo's own archive in the process (see page 178).

Kawakubo has now established a fashion empire to rival any of the more successful European conglomerates, but she has done so entirely on her own terms, refusing to compromise and constantly in search of that rare thing: the shock of the new. An unswervingly anarchic and trailblazing fashion institution – ask any other designer who is the most important force in modern fashion and they will almost invariably cite her name – she has applied this mindset not only to her twice-yearly women's and men's collections but also to print media, retail environments and, more recently, fragrance.

Kawakubo remains as intensely private, even wilfully elusive, as ever: 'This fascination with every nosy detail is astonishing. It would be much better to know someone through their work. With a singer, the best way is to listen to the song. For me, the best way to know me is to look at my clothing.'[3]

1. Deyan Sudjic, *Rei Kawakubo and Comme des Garçons*, New York (Rizzoli) 1990, p. 40.
2. Quoted in Susannah Frankel, 'Quiet Storm', *Independent Magazine*, September 2001.
3. *Ibid.*

Rei Kawakubo/Comme des Garçons
Spring/Summer 1997
Above: Top and skirt in stretch nylon/
polyurethane plain-weave printed gingham
check, with down pads
Opposite: Dress in stretch nylon/
polyurethane plain-weave printed gingham
check, with down pads

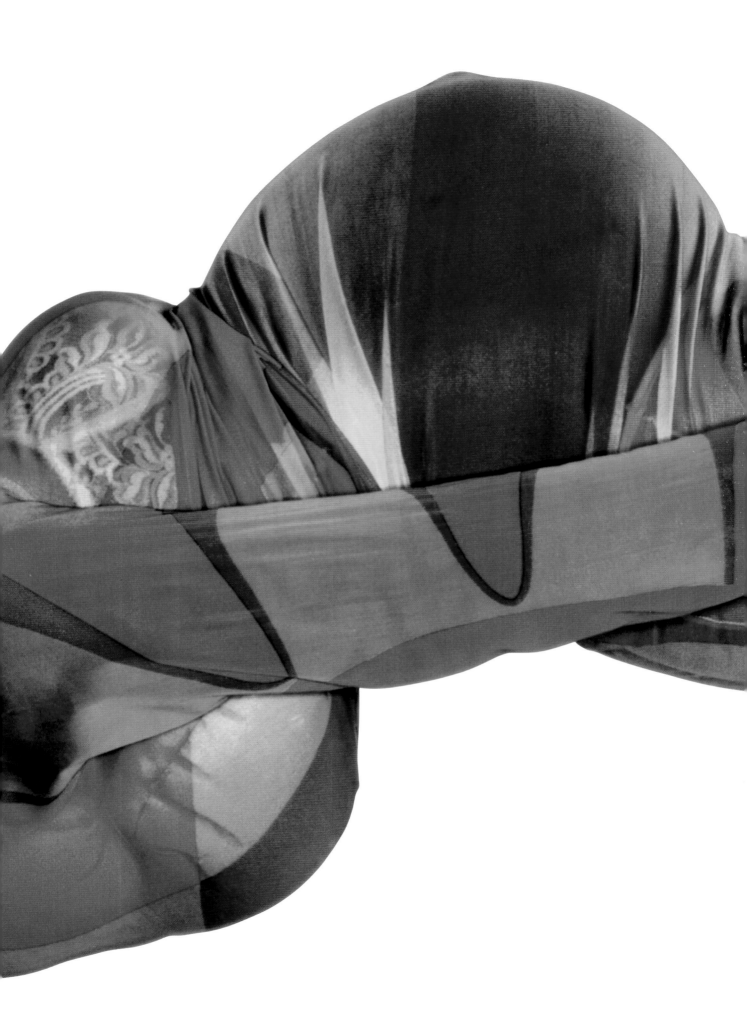

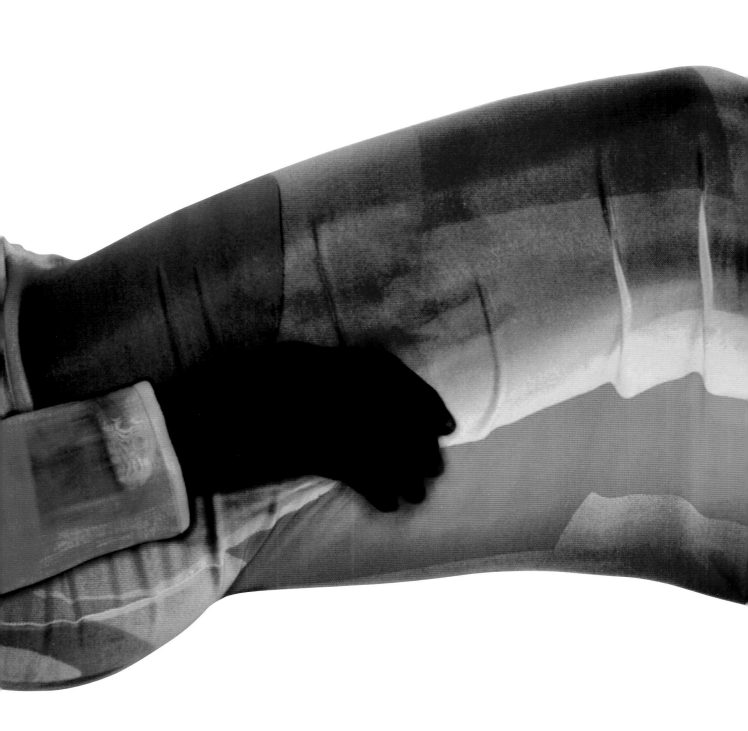

Pages 166–67, 168–69:
Rei Kawakubo/Comme des Garçons
Spring/Summer 1997
Photograph by Nick Knight
Art direction by Alexander McQueen
Styling by Katy England
Model Zoe Bedeaux
Published in *Visionaire 20: Comme des Garçons*, 1997

Opposite: *African Figure*, 1997
Linocut and monotype by François Berthoud
Published in Italian *Vogue*, 1997

Rei Kawakubo/Comme des Garçons
Autumn/Winter 1995–96
Above: Acrylic knitted sweater; matching
long skirt with embroidery, with knitted
bustle-like tube sewn to back of skirt;
tulle petticoat
Opposite: Catwalk presentation
Photograph by Niall McInerney

Overleaf: *Rei Kawakubo/Comme des Garçons*
Spring/Summer 2008
Left: Printed polyester twill coat, with
two bag pockets attached at front; yellow
cotton/polyester plain-weave trousers
Right: Purple polyester plain-weave coat
with large pouches inserted at waist; printed
cotton/polyester twill skirt, trimmed with
yellow cotton and polyester plain-weave
and yellow polyester tulle

The Comme des Garçons collection from
Spring/Summer 2008 (see overleaf), titled
'Cacophony', married motifs from a wide
range of disciplines, cultures and centuries.
At the catwalk show the music ranged from
circus whizz-bangs to rock 'n' roll and
traditional Japanese tunes, while anime
footage was projected on to the floor.
Patchwork was mixed with stripes, and
African-inspired prints with bloomer-like
frills. Faces were made up as sweet-shop-
coloured clowns. The double pea-coat on
page 174 has two large pockets – one stripy,

one dark grey. The coat's pattern, which
shows illustrations of braided hairstyles,
is a play on West African textiles, which
commonly depict such everyday modern
domestic objects as televisions and
telephones. The bold colour scheme of purple,
fuchsia, brown and white is complemented
by the vivid yellow of the trousers with
which it is teamed. These are a witty update
of modesty-preserving Victorian bloomers,
here subverted by the flamboyant hue and
missing panels that reveal rather than
conceal the wearer's legs.

Rei Kawakubo/Comme des Garçons
Spring/Summer 2010
Mixed materials sleeveless mini-dress

Deconstruction reigned at Comme des Garçons' Spring/Summer 2010 catwalk show, titled 'Tomorrow's Black'. This asymmetric sleeveless mini-dress is made of numerous small pieces of textile captured in a web of stitching. The shoulder areas of different tailored jackets were cut out, restructured and sewn back together to form protrusions in various places on the dress, reminiscent in conception of the 'Lumps and Bumps' of the 'Body Meets Dress, Dress Meets Body' collection of Spring/Summer 1997 yet very different in its meticulous construction. Fabrics in different colours, patterns and textures, including plain and flock-printed jacquard, velveteen and georgette covered in sequin embroidery, are brought together in exquisite harmony. Rei Kawakubo's unique sense of colour and exceptional skill in construction are clearly on display here. When asked backstage about the prominence of shoulder pads in the collection, she responded: 'I'm an adult delinquent, to the end.'[1]

1. Sarah Mower, 'Comme des Garçons', 3 October 2009, www.style.com/fashionshows/review/ S2010RTW-CMMEGRNS (accessed 30 May 2010).

Rei Kawakubo/Comme des Garçons
Spring/Summer 2010
Mixed materials long-trained skirt;
transparent nylon T-shirt; black
leather shoulder belt

YOHJI YAMAMOTO

Yohji Yamamoto is the most poetic of the great Japanese fashion designers. The roots of his aesthetic are buried deep in the tradition of workwear, referencing everything from the photography of August Sander to the industrial uniform of his native Japan, but as his career has progressed a more purely androgynous side has been played off against some of the most romantic and discreetly erotic designs in history.

Much time has been spent trying to unravel the mystery surrounding the man and his clothes by both pundits and devotees, of which there are many, fuelled at least in part by the designer's own elliptical commentary on his life and work: 'I think, people think "We still don't understand Yohji", he has said. 'I don't understand Yohji.'[1]

What is known about the designer is that he was born in Tokyo in 1943. His mother was a seamstress; his father was conscripted and killed in World War II. 'He went against his will', Yamamoto said in the documentary *Notebook on Cities and Clothes* (1989) directed by his friend Wim Wenders. 'When I think of my father, I realize that the war is still raging inside me.' After completing a degree in law at Keio University in Tokyo, Yamamoto turned his attention to fashion, working with his mother and graduating from Bunka Fashion College in the Japanese capital in 1969 before setting up as a designer in his own right.

Describing himself as a boy, Yamamoto has said: 'When friends of mine, schoolmates, invited me to go fishing or running in the mountains, I joined them but I didn't join them in their way. I was always watching. I didn't like myself.' At the same time, from a very early age he felt the need to express himself: 'I said to my friends "I am pushed. I have to express something." It was like somebody pushing my back. But I was a very quiet boy. I was always full of doubt.' The feeling continues to this day: 'It's difficult [for me] to doubt my main job.'

Like Rei Kawakubo, Yamamoto came to international prominence when he showed in Paris in 1981. Given that the two designers arrived on the Paris scene at the same time and demonstrated a similar interest in oversized, distressed garments that were almost unanimously black (even in Japan, women who chose to wear Yohji Yamamoto were labelled 'the crows'), it is unsurprising that they were grouped together, although neither felt entirely comfortable with that.

Despite any apparent similarity between their early collections, the two designers approach their work from entirely different viewpoints. For Yamamoto, a continuing love affair with black is intended to focus the viewer's attention on cut and proportion with no distraction. The shrouding of the body, meanwhile, famously springs from his experience of more crudely feminine attire at an early age: 'Where I was born,' he once said, 'there were very many prostitutes. They wore high heels and strong lipstick. And really, I was afraid. I was scared. Because they looked very, very wild. Not natural. I'm always trying to do something else, trying to find something else, trying to go somewhere else.'[2]

For some thirty years, then, Yamamoto has relied on the intimate relationship between garment and wearer over and above obvious high-impact effect and, certainly, status. In *Talking to Myself* (2002), a monograph dedicated to the designer's work, his friend Kiyokazu Washida, philosopher and professor at the Faculty of Literature at the graduate school of Osaka University, argues that Yamamoto's repeated description of his clothes as 'shabby' might be explained thus: 'What he means is that they do not allow association with any of society's particular stereotypes.' Whether they are worn by 'the salaried employee or the artist, the journalist or the student, the elderly or the young, his clothes are, in fact, difficult to match with any concrete image, when seen at a glance. Rather, in defiance of any such identification, they are in a sense peculiarly abstract.'[3]

Abstraction aside, however, Yamamoto's is an essentially humane approach. For example, far from proposing that women cover up any so-called imperfections, he positively revels in any asymmetry. For him it is a thing of beauty: 'I think perfection is ugly. Somewhere in the things humans make, I want to see scars, failure, disorder, distortion. If I can feel those things in works by others, then I like them. Perfection is a kind of order, like overall harmony and so on … They are things someone forces onto a thing. A free human being does not desire such things.'

1. Quoted in Susannah Frankel, 'Yohji Bared', *Independent on Sunday Review*, 11 August 2002. This is the source for all Yohji Yamamoto quotations in this section, unless otherwise indicated.
2. Quoted in Susannah Frankel, *Guardian Weekend Magazine*, September 1996.
3. Kiyokazu Washida, 'The Past, the Feminine, the Vain', in *Talking to Myself* by Yohji Yamamoto, Milan (Carla Sozzani) 2002, n.p.

Yohji Yamamoto
Spring/Summer 1998
Opposite: White silk/wool satin dress
with twisting
Above: Photograph by Inez van Lamsweerde
and Vinoodh Matadin
Art direction and design by M/M (Paris)
Overleaf: Photograph by Peter Lindbergh
Published in Italian *Vogue*, January 1998

Here Yohji Yamamoto transforms the
universal idea of the evening dress into
something light and contemporary. He has
followed the grain of the sensuous fabric
to create a supremely elegant dress with a
beautiful décolleté and train. No cuts or
darts were made, and the twisted fabric,
which wends continuously around the body,

is suggestive of the way a designer drapes
a garment on a dress form before the final
stages of completion.

The enigmatic Romanian model
Renée Perle – muse of acclaimed French
photographer Jacques Henri Lartigue –
inspired the collection, which, when shown,
transported the audience to 1930s Paris.

Yohji Yamamoto
Autumn/Winter 1996–97
Opposite: White wool felt dress;
black wool felt
Above: *Fashion 4*, 1996
Photograph by Sarah Moon

Yohji Yamamoto's clothes often combine
European dressmaking, workwear and
men's tailoring with a traditional Japanese
aesthetic. The silhouette seen here is a
constant feature in his designs: the result
of Yamamoto's principle of paring down a
garment to reveal what he calls 'the beauty
that remains after excess has been eliminated'.[1]
The notion of removing instead of adding is
central to the Japanese concept of *wabi-sabi*
(the aesthetics of the incomplete). While
the sculptural form cut away from the body's
natural contours is reminiscent of the
influential twentieth-century couturier
Cristóbal Balenciaga, the emphasis on the
back of the dress – achieved through its cut
and detailing – is akin to the attention given
to this area in kimono culture. As Yamamoto
has said: 'I think clothes should be made
from the back, and not the front. The back
supports the clothes, and so if it is not
properly made, the front cannot exist.'[2]

1. Quoted in Kiyokazu Washida, 'The Past, the
Feminine, the Vain', in *Talking to Myself* by Yohji
Yamamoto, Milan (Carla Sozzani) 2002, n.p.
2. *Ibid.*

Above: *Yohji Yamamoto*
Spring/Summer 1999
Quilted white polyester dress printed with grey
stripes and boned at the hem
Garden Party, 1998
Photograph by Sarah Moon

Overleaf: *Yohji Yamamoto*
Autumn/Winter 1997–98
Photograph by Annie Leibovitz
Published in American *Vogue*, September 1997

Opposite and above: *Yohji Yamamoto*
Autumn/Winter 2003–04
Black silk crêpe de Chine jacket with padded
cuffs; matching long skirt

Opposite and above: *Yohji Yamamoto*
Autumn/Winter 1985–86
Photographs by Paolo Roversi

Adidas/Yohji Yamamoto
Autumn/Winter 2001–02
Opposite: Navy-blue wool zip-opening
gaberdine jacket with inlay of light grey
lines instead of the right sleeve; matching
trousers combined with wrap skirt; black
nylon trainers with plastic white-lined
toes cover
Above: Catwalk presentation

Yohji Yamamoto has always used elements
of functional clothing in womenswear. He
collaborated with the German sporting
brand Adidas on this collection, and in the
outfit opposite the influence of the tracksuit
is evident, but in place of the right sleeve of
the jacket is a striped inlay, made of a fabric
that has little stretch, so that the right arm
is restricted. The outfit may be inspired by

sportswear but the design limits physical
movement. This conceptual playfulness
reflects Yamamoto's taste for cynical jokes
and his subtle mocking of the fashion industry.

In 2003 Yamamoto and Adidas launched
the much-coveted Y-3 line, which continues
to bring the designer's quirky take on modern
sportswear to the fast-moving world of urban
street fashion.

Yohji Yamamoto
Christina for 10, 2008
Photograph by Sarah Moon

JUNYA WATANABE

Born in Tokyo in 1961, Junya Watanabe graduated from Bunka Fashion College in 1984 and immediately went to work for Comme des Garçons. In 1987 he was made responsible for designing the Comme des Garçons Tricot line, and he introduced his first own-label collection in 1992. He has said that all he learned at fashion school 'was how to use a needle and thread and a sewing machine. Everything else I learned at Comme des Garçons.'[1]

Following in the footsteps of Comme des Garçons' founder Rei Kawakubo, Watanabe's immensely diverse output is unified in its dedication to the exploration of new concepts in cut, fabric and styling, remaining studiously out on a conceptual limb and purposefully oblivious of prevailing trends. And so, back in the early 1990s when he first showed under his own name and when international fashion appeared locked into minimalism, Watanabe sent out an entire collection of PVC clothing, which, in place of the ubiquitous monochrome and neutral colour palette, was, conversely, acid bright. Then came heavily tattooed, pale-faced models in black leather, and, not long after that, jewel-coloured brocade jackets over narrow, draped skirts. One season Watanabe might be inspired by mid-twentieth-century French haute couture – the Chanel bouclé wool suit and Courrèges boxy shift have both been given a barely recognizable makeover – the next he might make his entire collection out of waterproof fabrics and, just to prove it, shower his catwalk with rain (see page 209).

In more recent years, Watanabe has demonstrated an interest in American heritage clothing and denim in particular, collaborating with Levi Strauss to create more street-inspired designs. He applies just the same rigorous and complex approach to working with this most humble of fabrics as he does with any other.

Extreme styling and fashion-show pyrotechnics aside – glow-in-the-dark garments and models with bouquets of dried flowers tied to their heads or with their faces masked in studded black gaffer tape are just a few examples – it is perhaps Watanabe's highly intelligent and innovative study of apparently classic garments that stands out. Particularly remarkable is his exploration of men's tailoring and the trench coat innovatively re-evaluated to suit the feminine form. For the Spring/Summer 2010 season, for example, he sent out, without fanfare, an entire collection of tailored trouser suits, each one discreetly different from the next. This was an outstanding show, where subtlety more than the projection of an arresting image was the story. The silhouette was slender and deeply rooted in the menswear tradition, but still quintessentially feminine and curvaceous. Backs were cut away, pockets appeared at the sides of hips, shoulders were small and neat – and all with beautifully cut and equally narrow trousers to match (see pages 212–13).

'I have never thought about whether or not I am successful', Watanabe has said. 'Our aim is only to create a good collection. Every season, I think about what is necessary to express our creation in the strongest way possible and to leave the audience feeling that the clothes themselves are strong.'[2] Although fashion is a primarily commercial concern, there is little sense in Watanabe's work of kowtowing to the widely acknowledged tendency to slip at least one pair of relatively straightforward black trousers or an equally banal cashmere sweater into a selling collection. Instead, Watanabe designs his collections for a fashion-knowledgeable clientele and has no interest in his aesthetic being applauded on a more widespread basis.

'It's very simple', according to Watanabe, whose output seems anything but. 'I work hard to make the clothes I want to make and those who sympathize with my creation wear it. The people who buy my clothes take fashion seriously. They get a kick out of the challenge of wearing something new. Those are the people I design for. I am not interested in the mainstream.'[3]

1. Quoted in Susannah Frankel, 'Obscure Objects of Desire', *Guardian Weekend Magazine*, 15 August 1998.
2. Quoted in Susannah Frankel, *Dazed & Confused*, January 2003.
3. *Ibid.*

Junya Watanabe/Junya Watanabe Comme des Garçons
Spring/Summer 2003
Polychrome landscape-printed cotton plain-weave
dress; taped bags and large wired headgear of the same
fabric; white pad inside the bags

Junya Watanabe/
Junya Watanabe Comme des Garçons
Autumn/Winter 1998–99
White cotton plain-weave shirt-dress;
wired green wool serge skirt
Photograph by Anthea Simms

A masculine white shirt-dress is paired with a planar wool skirt in this characteristically uninhibited design from Junya Watanabe. In keeping with the theme of this collection, 'No Construction', dresses and skirts were given dimensionality by feeding coils of wire through the flat panels of fabric. At times the wire continued through the garment to coil round the model's neck, creating a piece of avant-garde jewellery. This circular skirt is particularly reminiscent of a Victorian hooped underskirt but is presented as outerwear.

Like his mentor, Rei Kawakubo, Watanabe refuses to reside in the world of convention, preferring to push the boundaries of construction and form with his experimental collections. His approach is, however, underpinned by an outstanding skill in traditional cutting techniques, and driven by a voracious appetite for ultra-modern fabrics and new textures.

Junya Watanabe/Junya Watanabe Comme des Garçons
Autumn/Winter 1998–99
Catwalk presentation

Junya Watanabe/
Junya Watanabe Comme des Garçons
Spring/Summer 2002
Opposite: Blue washed denim dress
Above: Photograph by Paolo Roversi
Fashion direction by Edward Enninful
Published in *i-D*, April 2002

With his exceptional cutting skill, Junya Watanabe has transformed an everyday piece of denim into an evening dress of remarkable elegance. The denim was washed to achieve a vintage-style suppleness and then skilfully cut to create the curves of the dress, which are accentuated by the stitching along the flounce. By combining bohemian fraying of the cut edges with a flowing silhouette, Watanabe has sublimated the high fashion–street fashion ambiguity of contemporary denim.

Junya Watanabe/Junya Watanabe Comme des Garçons
Spring/Summer 2001
Blue nylon/polyurethane plain-weave dress, trimmed
with blue acrylic resin circles

Junya Watanabe/Junya Watanabe Comme des Garçons
Spring/Summer 2000
Catwalk presentation

Junya Watanabe/Junya Watanabe Comme des Garçons
Autumn/Winter 2004–05
Orange, black, red and yellow padded polyester plain-
weave dress, wrapped at neck

Junya Watanabe/
Junya Watanabe Comme des Garçons
Spring/Summer 2010
Black polyester/cotton mix jacquard jacket
and trousers; black cotton broadcloth shirt

Junya Watanabe's neatly tailored trouser
suit emphasizes the curves of the waist and
hips. Curvilinear darts at the sides make the
jacket jut forward at the hip, while a sharp
split detail at the back of the collar adds an
unusual individuality and highlights the
erotic zone of the neck and back. These details
– a perfect blend of experimentation and
utility – add a touch of the designer's
signature distinctiveness to a classic staple
of the working woman's wardrobe. The
collection's two-tone footwear and tonic-
style suiting bring to mind the sharply
tailored mods of 1960s Britain.

JUN TAKAHASHI

Jun Takahashi's Undercover label is notable for being indebted to the culture of street fashion while drawing on references as diverse as floral bouquets, Stanley Kubrick's A Clockwork Orange *(1971), taxidermy and Japanese manga cartoons. If the latter seem disparate, they are united by the fact that they are, almost invariably, dark.*

Takahashi is based in Tokyo but, since 2002 and the Spring/Summer 2003 season, the label has been shown in Paris. At Takahashi's debut collection, Comme des Garçons' Rei Kawakubo took pride of place in the front row – quite an endorsement and one driven home by the fact that it was, by all accounts, Kawakubo who first encouraged the designer to show there.

Born in Kiryu, Gunma prefecture, in 1969, Takahashi studied fashion at Tokyo's Bunka Fashion College. He graduated in 1991 and opened a shop called Nowhere two years later, dividing the space between himself and his friend and fellow student Tomoaki 'Nigo' Nagao, today known for heading up the cult label A Bathing Ape.

Takahashi is almost fanatically devoted to the Sex Pistols – his appearance has been compared to John Lydon and, as a student, he fronted a tribute band – and he clearly embraces a similarly anarchic point of view. A certain gothicism also pervades his aesthetic ('Maybe in a past life I was a goth, living in a castle, somewhere crazy'[1]), as does deconstructivism – raw edges are always much in evidence. While sources of inspiration might shift on a seasonal basis, at the heart of the matter is heavily worked clothing that is patched, layered, slashed and printed with bold graphics and that impressively fuses anarchy with elegance as if it were the most natural thing in the world.

Takahashi works from his Tokyo-based design studio, entitled the 'Undercoverlab' and designed by Klein Dytham architecture in 2001. Undercover stores are unified by the fact that they are just that: little light is allowed to penetrate, only adding to any insider kudos that surrounds the name.

'What about the clothes?' wondered the *International Herald Tribune*'s Suzy Menkes in 2006: 'They are beautifully crafted and pretty in a weird way. The spring collection, shown at the crumbling Bouffes du Nord theatre in Paris, had layers of tablecloth lightness, with insides spilling out as if from a doll's stomach. Another show had feathers intricately cut out in felt. For winter the wrappings included a white jacket bandaged with ties, the headpiece decorated with rings and chains where eyes and nose should be.'[2]

The designer himself has claimed that his work treads the fine line between the beautiful and the ugly. In truth, while there is generally a somewhat macabre element to his clothes, to the Undercover devotee – and there are many – the beautiful generally dominates.

1. Jun Takahashi, quoted in Susie Rushton, 'A Shocking Talent', *The Independent*, 31 July 2006.
2. Suzy Menkes, 'Strange but Beautiful', *International Herald Tribune*, 11 April 2006.

Jun Takahashi/Undercover
Autumn/Winter 2000–01
Jacket, sweater, skirt, trousers, scarf, belt,
bag, gloves, stockings and wig of various
fabrics including wool, mohair and synthetic
'leather', painted, printed and embroidered
with tartan pattern

Jun Takahashi/Undercover
Autumn/Winter 2000–01
Brown jacket, top, skirt, scarf, gloves and
boots of various fabrics including wool,
cotton and rayon/polyester, printed with
black dot pattern

Jun Takahashi/Undercover
Autumn/Winter 2000–01
Camel jacket, skirt, gloves, stockings,
belt and shoes of various fabrics including
leather, suede and wool

Jun Takahashi/Undercover
Autumn/Winter 2000–01
Jacket, sweater, skirt, scarf, belt, gloves
and stockings of various fabrics including
wool, cotton, leather and blended fabric,
woven, embroidered and printed with
polychrome floral pattern

Each of the tailored parts of this suit is made
from a variety of different fabrics, all patterned
with flowers. Sequins sewn on to the
wallpaper-like pattern glisten like dewdrops
on a rose. The scarf and belt are decorated
with beading. The pattern continues on
stockings and shoes and, when the collection
was shown on the catwalk, the models' faces
and wigs were painted with the same floral
pattern. Such characteristic Takahashi
finishes as fraying and unfinished edges
are visible throughout.

Other ensembles from Jun Takahashi's
inventive Autumn/Winter 2000–01
'Melting Pot' collection were produced
in caramel leather and lace, dark brown
wool and cotton printed with black spots
(see pages 219 and 221), or all-over tartan
(see page 217). A tartan pleated skirt-over-
trousers outfit borrowed from the sartorial
language of punk, but Takahashi added
subtle and luxurious embellishments, such
as neat rows of silver sequins along the pale
grid lines of the check trousers.

TAO KURIHARA

Although born in Tokyo in 1973 and now showing her collections twice yearly in the world's fashion capital, Paris, Tao Kurihara in fact trained in London at Central Saint Martins College. 'I couldn't find any Japanese universities and colleges where I could investigate my interests more deeply. I think I learned self-motivation and independence from Central Saint Martins,' she has said.[1] Her career path since that time, however, is indebted to Comme des Garçons. After graduating, she worked there as assistant to Junya Watanabe and also designed the Comme des Garçons Tricot line. Although Kurihara has never worked directly with Rei Kawakubo, she says she learned 'the spirit of creation' from her mentor, even going so far as to claim that her interest in fashion has its roots in this formidable source.

When asked whether her Japanese heritage has any influence over her design sensibility, Kurihara has argued that this is, at least in part and with certain reservations, inevitable:

I don't deny that my national identity is reflected in my work. I think I'm influenced by the environment where I grew up and especially by my experience at Comme des Garçons. However, I don't think my way of working would change if I was another nationality, my standpoint would still be the same. It's simply that one can't help but be influenced by the way one has grown up and the place where one happens to live. Nationality is just pure chance.

Despite a clarity of intent and perhaps because of her extreme reverence towards Kawakubo, Kurihara's first reaction to the launching of her own line (Tao Comme des Garçons) for the Autumn/Winter 2005–06 season was '99 per cent fear! In the beginning I felt "no way" but I jumped through the door that Rei Kawakubo opened for me with only one per cent of hope because I thought it was a really good opportunity and challenge for me.' She has risen to this challenge beautifully.

From a critically acclaimed debut featuring elaborately knitted lingerie to collections focusing on everything from trench coats and handkerchiefs to wedding dresses and from 1980s-inspired sportswear to blankets and stoles, it is clear that self-imposed limitations are central to this designer's signature, allowing her to explore a single precise idea fully: 'I was attracted to the strong, cool, definite form of trench coats,' she has said of the Spring/Summer 2006 collection, 'but I wanted to make something very different from traditional, water-resistant and functional trenches. So I chose to work with something fragile and familiar: handkerchiefs. The collection is mostly white, because, to me, the image of the most beautiful handkerchief is versions of white.'

Of the collection of wedding dresses shown a year later (Spring/Summer 2007; see pages 100–101) she has said:

What attracts me most is how special the wedding dress is. That is because it is worn only once. Some people get married a few times but they don't, I would imagine, wear the same outfit or go on to wear their wedding dress again as part of their daily wardrobe. Paper is so fragile and not appropriate for overuse. I thought a paper wedding dress would be more special than one that was crafted out of a more traditional and typically extravagant material.

If Kurihara shares with both Kawakubo and Watanabe a passion for individuality at whatever cost, it is worth noting that this is increasingly a rarity: 'I don't really mind about what trends are. My creation has to be very individual, therefore I don't make clothes that people like, rather I make clothes that I think are beautiful.'

1. All quotations are from Susannah Frankel, 'Unbridled Classic', *The Independent*, 2 April 2007, and 'The Paper Tiger Roars', *The Independent*, 14 October 2007.

Tao Kurihara/Tao Comme des Garçons
Spring/Summer 2009
Blue polyester organdie pleated jacket,
with brandenburgs at front; black-and-
white-striped cotton jersey cropped trousers;
grey knitted socks with fringes

Above: Scrapbook by fashion observer/ illustrator Lele Acquarone published in Italian *Vogue*, April 2009

Overleaf, left: *Tao Kurihara/ Tao Comme des Garçons* Spring/Summer 2009 Print by Rúna Thorkelsdottir

Overleaf, right: *Tao Kurihara/ Tao Comme des Garçons* Spring/Summer 2009 Polychrome polyester plain-weave jacket, printed with tulip pattern and trimmed with floral-patterned lace, with brandenburgs at front and bell-shaped buttons; cropped trousers of the same fabric; black knitted socks with fringes Print by Rúna Thorkelsdottir

Tao Kurihara/Tao Comme des Garçons
Autumn/Winter 2006–07
Pink-dyed overdress of various fabrics;
purple-dyed dress of silk/cotton fabrics;
both trimmed with various coloured fabrics

Tao Kurihara/Tao Comme des Garçons
Autumn/Winter 2006–07
Catwalk presentation

Tao Kurihara's abundant wrapping and layering of stoles and dresses in the pieces shown opposite and above create soft, voluminous forms and cloak the wearer in pretty, petal-like frills. The collection, called 'Stoles and Flowers', featured a plethora of tie-dyed capes, wraps, loose trousers, dresses and, of course, stoles, all trimmed with ruffles, lace or floral corsages and in an ultra-feminine palette of neutral and pastel shades occasionally mixed with edgier black. Every season Kurihara reassembles and reinterprets existing shapes and decorative techniques from scratch, imbuing the new garments with her own unique vision. Each of her collections, revered by fashion journalists, offers a singular aesthetic and is delivered with a confidence belied by the overwhelming sweetness of her designs.

Tao Kurihara/Tao Comme des Garçons
Spring/Summer 2010
White overdress in strands of synthetic fabric; sheer black tunic

For this collection Tao Kurihara set herself the challenge of producing clothes without sewing. The sheer black tunic is overlaid with an equally diaphanous white dress made of layers of finely torn pieces of fabric that have been twisted and knotted into shape using a technique similar to macramé. Large gaps between the knots leave most of the body uncovered and give the dress the look of an oversized decorative accessory made from string.

The dress is meticulously put together and exudes the warmth of the hand-crafted. Yet this piece and the one shown opposite both possess a directness and attitude that is a world away from homely craft and closer to the rebellious spirit of DIY punk style. These tensions and contradictions are what make Kurihara's conceptual creations so captivating.

Tao Kurihara/Tao Comme des Garçons
Spring/Summer 2010
Black overdress in strands of synthetic fabric;
sheer black tunic

THE NEXT GENERATION

Hirofumi Kurino

It was March 2010 and Paris Fashion Week was in full swing. The Moncler flagship store was filled with the products of the French label's project 'Moncler S', the 'S' standing for Sacai, the independent Japanese label launched in 1999 by Chitose Abe, designer of this collaborative range (see page 240). From humble beginnings, with Abe presenting three sample styles to potential clients in her living room, Sacai now has stockists worldwide. Its clients are all multi-label stores, such as London's Dover Street Market, which gather together top brands reflecting a particular fashion preference. The success of Sacai – a label that does not do runway shows or put out any advertising as such, that until recently had staged only simple displays to showcase its collection and that has developed without any major financial backing – offers clues for understanding the phenomenon of 'Cool Japan', and in particular what makes Japanese fashion brands so unconventional in their creative processes and approach to business.

After studying fashion at Nagoya Fashion College, Abe worked for Comme des Garçons on its Tricot line, a consistent performer in the label's stable. Word has it that Abe was known as the queen of separates because everything she made simply flew off the shelves. Her knits in particular are deceptively simple yet with superb detailing that fashion followers find irresistible. These are pieces designed for everyday wear, but with an extra whiff of design X-factor that creates an added value not found in the knits of other labels or those of the low-cost, high-volume fast fashion currently dominating the global apparel market. Nor are Abe's designs prohibitively expensive. She is an enthusiastic fashion consumer herself, and underpinning her creativity is a healthy hold on reality: 'This is worth buying at this price'; 'I can wear it with that outfit I already have, day and night.'

Sacai's clothes are manufactured with an eye to such realities, and the company's sound business approach is arguably inherited from Comme des Garçons' Rei Kawakubo, who is something of a mentor to the young designer. Other designers have followed similar paths: Kazuaki Takashima of Né-net (see pages 246–47) and Tamae Hirokawa, the designer behind Somarta (see page 245), perfected their fashion skills and business acumen under Issey Miyake as designers of the 'Pleats Please' collection and main and menswear lines respectively.

Among another group of emerging Japanese designers, it is impossible to overlook the influence of street culture or the aesthetic and creative compulsions of *otaku* (manga and anime obsessives). The influence of globalization and the Internet – in particular, blogging and tweeting – is clearly evident in the work of some, for whom the important thing is to communicate a message rather than create new forms. For his Spring/Summer 2008 'Industrial Dolls' collection, Mikio Sakabe (see page 237) took as inspiration the ordinary – yet, precisely because of its ordinariness, extraordinary – doll-like quality of the white-collar female workers known in Japan as 'office ladies', or 'OLs': 'I wanted to take something that is as un-individualistic as an office uniform and show that a woman can still be fashionably unique despite wearing something that may seem to be the antithesis of individuality. And I also find the uniform to be feminine but sexually demure at the same time', Sakabe has said.[1]

To preceding generations, fashion represented the pinnacle of value creation, and designers expressed their originality by coming up with new forms and silhouettes, through the use of colour, materials and detailing. Today's designers give concept and message precedence over formalism. It is interesting to note that many of the designers now working in Japan trained in Europe – a cultural exchange clearly evident in their work. Sakabe, Akira Naka (see page 238) and Taro Horiuchi (see page 239) all studied at Antwerp's Royal Academy of Fine Arts, which has one of the world's pre-eminent fashion departments, alma mater of the likes of Martin Margiela and the 'Antwerp Six'.[2] Teaching there is based on hammering in to students the importance of 'concept' over technical qualities. Horiuchi's ethereal and reductive Spring/Summer 2010 collection inspired by 'faith, nature and time' is nonetheless exquisitely tailored and detailed. Similarly, Naka's edgy take on tailoring that fades into knitwear works not only because of its conceptual freshness but also, crucially, because of the designer's precision and technique.

Other designers, such as Hokuto Katsui and Nao Yagi of mintdesigns (see page 243) and Tao Kurihara of Tao Comme des Garçons, are products of the renowned fashion course at Central Saint Martins College in London. Kurihara (see pages 225–33) could be described as the designer of the Comme des Garçons stable closest in spirit to Rei Kawakubo. Like Kawakubo and Saint Martins alumni John Galliano and Alexander McQueen, Kurihara possesses both a talent for creating arresting concepts and the skills to give those concepts concrete expression. Mintdesigns' strong signature style is heavily – almost fetishistically – based on print and graphics. Their source material, from newsprint and cult American graphic novels to building blueprints, runs through their choice of catwalk venue, the look of their invitations and packaging, and even the materials and techniques employed in their garments and accessories.

On a wet day in October 2009 in a disused elementary school in a working-class district of Tokyo, a world away from the milieu of high fashion, writtenafterwards (Yoshikazu Yamagata) unveiled a collection inspired by the gods of Greek myth and legend. Elderly models wearing single pieces of cloth in various styles sashayed down the catwalk as if walking on clouds. Was this a joke or was there a serious message? Was it to be seen as an attempt to show the sort of clothing that can be created with a single piece of cloth, or as a shrewdly ironic comment on a fashion system in which whatever appears on the catwalk is deemed 'sacred'? Whatever the show's intended message, the capacity crowd assembled that day witnessed a kind of creativity peculiar to Tokyo designers. This was not about simply churning out fashionable fashion or cheap fashion, or recruiting 'slebs' as accomplices in calculated media manipulations to raise a designer's profile among the masses: this was fashion post-subprime, post-fast fashion, post-celebrity hype value.

Was the 'Gods' collection a product of some determination to find value in fashion despite these tendencies? It would seem so. This new generation of Japanese designers is commenting on the very contemporary issue of our consumerist society and where it might lead us in the future. Little wonder the fashion world continues to fascinate.

1. Quoted in Misha Janette and Paul McInnes, 'Sizing up the Season's Hot Pick of Japan's Finest Couture', *Japan Times*, 23 March 2008.

2. The Antwerp Six graduated from the city's Royal Academy of Fine Arts between 1980 and 1981 and are: Walter Van Beirendonck, Dirk Bikkembergs, Ann Demeulemeester, Dries Van Noten, Dirk Van Saene and Marina Yee.

Mikio Sakabe
Spring/Summer 2008, 'Industrial Dolls' collection

AKIRA NAKA

Akira Naka
Autumn/Winter 2009–10
Grey wool jacket with gradation knit; white
acetate/polyester knitted top; black lamé
polyester knitted leggings

Akira Naka studied fashion design at Bunka
Fashion College in Tokyo and the Royal
Academy of Fine Arts in Antwerp before
establishing his fashion label in 2008. Naka
specializes in innovative knitwear, and his
recent collections have blended knitting
techniques with sharply tailored details.
His Autumn/Winter 2009–10 collection
featured blazers and pencil skirts edged
with cable knit.

TARO HORIUCHI

Taro Horiuchi
Spring/Summer 2010
White polyester organdie dress, coated with
washi (Japanese paper); overdress made of
very thin polyester organdie

Taro Horiuchi graduated from Antwerp
Royal Academy of Fine Arts in 2007 and
established his own label in 2009. Horiuchi
has described his designs as 'super minimal',
believing that this approach serves to
highlight the beauty of the people who
wear his clothes.

SACAI

Chitose Abe/Sacai
Spring/Summer 2010
Top: White rayon/polyester jersey T-shirt
with silk chiffon ornament; cotton/silk skirt
with cupra chiffon pleats at both sides of
waist; cotton/cupra tulle cuffs
Above: Grey cotton/polyester jacket with
rayon/nylon lace and silk chiffon trimming,
and polyester net inside; grey cotton/
polyester shorts

Chitose Abe established the label Sacai in
1999, having worked previously with Junya
Watanabe at Comme des Garçons. Abe often
chooses to combine a number of different
fabrics, using lace, satin and chiffon within
a single piece. She has revisited the same
silhouette for the past few seasons, creating
mini-skirts and shorts teamed with casual
T-shirts and cropped zipped jackets.

MINÄ PERHONEN

Minä Perhonen
Spring/Summer 2008
Dress of woven strings of black leather,
with mother-of-pearl work

Akira Minagawa established the label Minä
Perhonen (meaning 'I butterfly' in Finnish)
in Tokyo in 1995. He showed his first
collection outside Japan in 2004 and opened
his first shop in 2007 in Kyoto. Minagawa
became inspired by Finnish aesthetics after
travelling in Scandinavia, and his early
collections were influenced by Nordic folk
costume. As well as designing garments,
Minagawa creates original textiles and
furniture, and his most recent collections
have included simple clothes constructed
from his own printed cottons.

MIKIO SAKABE

Mikio Sakabe
Autumn/Winter 2008–09
Yellow wool/nylon melton short coat
with long muffler

Mikio Sakabe met his design partner and
now wife Shueh Jen-Fang while studying at
the Royal Academy of Fine Arts in Antwerp,
and they formed the label Mikio Sakabe
together in Tokyo in 2006. The couple are
especially interested in advanced textile
technology and often incorporate innovative
fabrics in their collections. In recent
presentations they have styled their models
as living dolls: the models at their Autumn/
Winter 2008–09 catwalk show appeared as
life-size Licca dolls (Japanese Barbies)
wearing sci-fi-inspired skirt and trouser
suits teamed with oversized scarves and
cropped duffel coats.

MINTDESIGNS

mintdesigns
Autumn/Winter 2009–10
Purple and white plain-weave cotton dress;
navy-blue wool flannel trousers with
embroidery; navy-blue knitted gloves
with white polka dots

Hokuto Katsui and Nao Yagi met while
studying fashion design at Central Saint
Martins College in London, and formed
the womenswear and childrenswear label
mintdesigns together in Tokyo in 2001.
Mintdesigns' work is characterized by
lightness, delicacy and a special fondness
for printed motifs. In 2007 they used
paper-chain dolls as a recurring motif
for a collection of lace skirts and shawls.

ANREALAGE

Anrealage
Autumn/Winter 2008–09
Black wool/polyester plain-weave dress
with decoration of polystyrene beads

Kunihiko Morinaga graduated from Waseda
University, Tokyo, and Vantan Design
Institute before launching his label Anrealage
(a combination of the words 'real', 'unreal'
and 'age') in 2003. Morinaga has an avant-
garde approach to fashion, and his designs
frequently explore clothing in relation to
form. For Spring/Summer 2009 his clothing
was shown on geometrical forms before
being peeled off and then placed on human
bodies, while his Spring/Summer 2010
collection presented the garments only
as black silhouettes on a light board.

SOMARTA

Somarta
Spring/Summer 2010
Red rayon/nylon knitted bodice with
ornaments of silk flower petals; purple
nylon/polyester knitted skirt

Tamae Hirokawa graduated from Bunka
Fashion College in 1998 and worked initially
under Issey Miyake before establishing
Somarta, her own fashion label, in 2007.
Much like her mentor, Hirokawa is
fascinated by the potential of advances
in textile technology. Her creations are
always richly embellished and highly
decorated: her Spring/Summer 2010
collection combined elasticized lace
bodysuits with a profusion of silk petals.

NÉ-NET

Né-net
Autumn/Winter 2009–10

Kazuaki Takashima graduated from Bunka Fashion College in Tokyo in 1994 and joined Issey Miyake in 1996. He worked initially as chief designer for Miyake's 'Pleats Please' collection, and launched his own label, Né-net, under the umbrella of A-net Inc., Miyake's sister company, in 2005. Known for his bright, innovative and satirical designs, Takashima takes inspiration from the dark nuances and sentiments of modern Japanese youth culture.

Inspired by the Japanese concept of *Muteki ni naritai* ('hero nostalgia'), the catwalk show for Autumn/Winter 2009–10 was held in a ring in Tokyo's Korukuen Hall, where professional boxing and wrestling matches are held. The models entered the ring wearing colourful masks, gloves and boots like boxers or wrestlers, to a backing track of the presidential oath given by the US president, Barack Obama.

1

2

3

4

9

10

11

12

1970
Kenzo Takada opens his first clothing store, Jungle Jap, in Paris. (**1**)
Issey Miyake launches the Miyake Design Studio in Tokyo.

1971
Issey Miyake holds his first overseas collection in New York.
Pioneering French fashion designer Gabrielle 'Coco' Chanel dies.

1972
Yohji Yamamoto establishes his own fashion label.
Spanish fashion designer Cristóbal Balenciaga dies.
The Italian fashion label Missoni reaches the height of its popularity.
Diane Von Furstenberg is made famous for her wrap dresses and her motto, 'Feel like a woman. Wear a dress.'

1973
The governing body of the French fashion industry, the Fédération française de la couture, du prêt-à-porter des couturiers et des créateurs de mode, is established.
Issey Miyake shows his collection in Paris for the first time.
Rei Kawakubo founds the Japanese label Comme des Garçons.
Halston sells his brand to Norton Industries and begins to define 1970s disco fashion with his designs.

1974
Thierry Mugler launches his own label, which becomes known for close-fitting and square shoulder style in the 1980s.

1975
Milan Fashion Week is founded.
Rei Kawakubo presents her first collection in Tokyo.
Issey Miyake opens his first shop in Paris.

1976
Jean Paul Gaultier debuts his collection in Paris.
Influential French designer Yves Saint Laurent introduces the 'peasant look'.
Paul Smith debuts his menswear collection in Paris.
Vivienne Westwood and Malcolm McLaren open Seditionaries in London (following on from their earlier shops, Let It Rock, Too Fast to Live Too Young to Die and SEX) and pave the way for punk fashion. (**2**)

1977
Yohji Yamamoto debuts his collection in Tokyo.
Issey Miyake displays 'A Piece of Cloth' at Seibu Museum of Art, Tokyo.
The nightclub Studio 54 opens in New York.
Hanae Mori becomes the first Asian woman to be admitted to the Chambre syndicale de la haute couture in Paris. (**3**)

1978
Issey Miyake establishes his menswear line, and the book *Issey Miyake: East Meets West* is published.
Comme des Garçons establishes the menswear line Homme.
Gianni Versace opens his first boutique in Milan.

1979
Calvin Klein causes controversy with the provocative tag-line: 'You know what gets between me and my Calvins? Nothing.'

1980
Tunisian-born Azzedine Alaïa debuts his collection in Paris and introduces his 'body-conscious' aesthetic.
The flamboyant and colourful clothing of the New Romantics scene provides an alternative style to the prevailing punk trend.
Stephen Jones establishes himself as a leading British milliner.
The Italian fashion label Armani becomes the leading menswear brand after Richard Gere wears its garments in the film *American Gigolo*. (**4**)

1981
Yohji Yamamoto and Rei Kawakubo make their Paris debuts.
The Antwerp Six graduate from Antwerp's Royal Academy of Fine Arts: Walter Van Beirendonck, Dirk Bikkembergs, Ann Demeulemeester, Dries Van Noten, Dirk Van Saene and Marina Yee.
David and Elizabeth Emanuel design Princess Diana's wedding dress. (**5**)

CHRONOLOGY

5

6

7

8

13

14

15

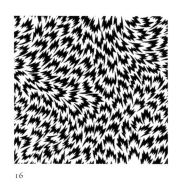

16

1982

Vivienne Westwood debuts her collection in Paris.

Rei Kawakubo opens her first shop in Paris.

Yohji Yamamoto's and Rei Kawakubo's Spring/ Summer 1983 collections cause a media sensation referred to as 'Japan shock'. (**6**)

1983

Yohji Yamamoto opens his first shop in Paris.

Karl Lagerfeld is appointed chief designer for Chanel.

Katharine Hamnett wears one of her political T-shirts with the slogan '58% Don't Want Pershing' at a meeting with the British prime minister, Margaret Thatcher. (**7**)

1984

John Galliano's final degree show at Central Saint Martins College of Art and Design, London. (**8**)

Junya Watanabe joins Comme des Garçons.

London Fashion Week is launched.

1985

The Council of Fashion Designers, Tokyo, is founded and the twice-yearly Tokyo Collection (now called Japan Fashion Week) is established.

Donna Karan launches her label and goes on to define minimalist fashion in the 1990s.

Tommy Hilfiger launches his label.

1986

Domenico Dolce and Stefano Gabbana debut their collection in Milan.

Japanese Avant-Garde 1910–1970 exhibition at the Centre Pompidou in Paris.

Issey Miyake begins a long collaboration with celebrated photographer Irving Penn.

1987

Italian label Balenciaga is rebranded as a ready-to-wear label.

The seminal exhibition *Three Women* is presented at the Fashion Institute of Technology, New York, and features clothing by Madeleine Vionnet, Claire McCardell and Rei Kawakubo. (**9**)

Junya Watanabe is appointed head designer for Comme des Garçons' knitwear line, Tricot.

Louis Vuitton and Moët Hennessy merge to form the LVMH group.

1988

Martin Margiela debuts his collection in Paris.

Prada creates a ready-to-wear collection.

Comme des Garçons launches the biannual magazine *Six* (1988–91).

Anna Wintour is appointed editor-in-chief of American *Vogue*.

1989

Wim Wenders directs a documentary on Yohji Yamamoto entitled *Notebook on Cities and Clothes*.

Philip Treacy secures Isabella Blow as one of his enthusiastic patrons.

1990

Jean Paul Gaultier designs the conical bra for Madonna's Blond Ambition tour.

The Wonderbra gains worldwide success. (**10**)

Koji Tatsuno debuts his collection in Paris. (**11**)

Jun Takahashi founds label Undercover while at fashion college, and formally establishes it as a company a few years later. (**12**)

1991

Issey Miyake is commissioned to design the stage sets and costumes for *The Loss of Small Detail* for William Forsythe's Ballet Frankfurt. (**13**)

1992

Junya Watanabe launches his label Junya Watanabe Comme des Garçons in Tokyo.

Viktor Horsting and Rolf Snoeren launch the Viktor & Rolf fashion house. (**14**)

Marc Jacobs brings grunge to the runway with his collection for Perry Ellis.

British style magazine *Dazed & Confused* is launched.

Hiroaki Ohya graduates from the Bunka Fashion College, Tokyo, and joins the Miyake Design Studio. (**15**)

Wakako Kishimoto and Mark Eley establish the label Eley Kishimoto. (**16**)

Miuccia Prada launches the Miu Miu line.

Alexandra Shulman is appointed editor-in-chief of British *Vogue*.

Alexander McQueen graduates from Central Saint Martins College of Art and Design, London, and fashion editor Isabella Blow purchases his entire collection.

Picture details are on page 254.

17

18

19

20

25

26

27

28

1993

Issey Miyake experiments with new methods
of pleating, culminating in the launch of
the 'Pleats Please' line. (**17**)
Vivienne Westwood launches her more
affordable Anglomania label.
John Galliano debuts his collection in Paris.
Hussein Chalayan causes a sensation with
his graduate collection of decomposed
silk dresses. (**18**)

1994

Tom Ford is appointed creative director
of Gucci.
Marc Jacobs launches his own label.

1995

Hubert de Givenchy retires and John
Galliano is appointed chief designer
for the Givenchy fashion house. (**19**)
Dai Fujiwara joins the Miyake Design Studio.
Alexander McQueen's low-rise Bumster
trousers initiate the trend for low-rise jeans.
Raf Simons launches his menswear label.

1996

Hiroaki Ohya debuts his label Ohya in Paris.
Alexander McQueen replaces John Galliano
as chief designer for Givenchy.
John Galliano produces his first couture
collection as chief designer for
Christian Dior.

1997

Choreographer Merce Cunningham
produces *Scenario*, with costumes and
stage sets by Rei Kawakubo. (**20**)
Nicolas Ghesquière is appointed head
designer for Balenciaga.
Marc Jacobs is appointed creative director
of Louis Vuitton and creates the label's
first ready-to-wear line.
Viktor & Rolf debut their haute couture
collection (Spring/Summer 1998).
Julien MacDonald and Matthew Williamson
debut at London Fashion Week.
Stella McCartney is appointed creative
director of Chloé.
Gianni Versace is murdered and his sister
Donatella Versace is appointed head
designer for the clothing range.
Avant-garde designer Jeremy Scott launches
his collection.

1998

Tao Kurihara joins Comme des Garçons.
Sex and the City's costume designer, Patricia
Field, makes the cast's wardrobe an
international fashion guide.
Issey Miyake launches the 'A-POC' concept. (**21**)

1999

Kenzo Takada retires from his brand but the
label continues.
Naoki Takizawa is appointed design director
of Issey Miyake's mainline collection.
Chitose Abe sets up the label Sacai. (**22**)

2000

Yohji Yamamoto's daughter, Limi, makes
her debut in Tokyo.
Hussein Chalayan's autumn/winter
collection merges fashion and architecture
with cantilevered dresses that turn into
furniture. (**23**)
Philip Treacy is invited to present the first
ever haute couture show of hats in Paris.

2001

Junya Watanabe launches his menswear line.
Julien MacDonald replaces Alexander
McQueen as chief designer for Givenchy.
Christopher Bailey is appointed creative
director of Burberry Prorsum.
Stella McCartney resigns from Chloé to set
up her own label.
Hokuto Katsui and Nao Yagi found Japanese
fashion label mintdesigns. (**24**)
Hedi Slimane is appointed head designer for
Dior Homme.
Alber Elbaz is appointed artistic director
of France's oldest couture house, Lanvin.
Zac Posen debuts his collection in New York.

2002

mintdesigns debut in Tokyo.
Yves Saint Laurent retires.
Yohji Yamamoto debuts his haute couture
collection in Paris.
Undercover debuts in Paris.
Dolce & Gabbana purchase Richard Nicoll's
entire graduate collection.

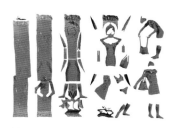

21

22

23

24

29

30

31

32

2003

Jean Paul Gaultier replaces Martin Margiela as creative director of Hermès.

Topshop sponsors Fashion East, a non-profit-making project to showcase emerging young fashion designers.

Jonathan Saunders debuts at London Fashion Week.

Marc Jacobs collaborates with artist Takashi Murakami to update Louis Vuitton's traditional monogram and create a range of accessories for the brand.

2004

Giles Deacon debuts his collection at London Fashion Week.

Tom Ford resigns as head designer for Yves Saint Laurent and is replaced by Stefano Pilati.

2005

Tom Ford launches his own label.

Gareth Pugh debuts at Fashion East. (**25**)

The 'Stella McCartney for H&M' collection sells out worldwide.

Tao Kurihara shows her first independent collection in Paris under the label Tao Comme des Garçons. (**26**)

2006

Matohu debuts at Japan Fashion Week. (**27**)

London-based Carri Mundane establishes her new label, Cassette Playa. (**28**)

Christopher Kane graduates from London's Central Saint Martins College of Art and Design, and is offered a consultancy position with Donatella Versace.

Phoebe Philo resigns as creative director of Chloé.

Henry Holland catapults to fame with his Katharine Hamnett-inspired T-shirts displaying tongue-in-cheek slogans about members of the fashion industry. (**29**)

Tamae Hirokawa establishes the Tokyo label Somarta after eight years under Issey Miyake.

2007

Dai Fujiwara is appointed creative director of Issey Miyake.

Magazine editor and international style icon Isabella Blow commits suicide. (**30**)

2008

Yves Saint Laurent dies.

Gareth Pugh debuts his collection in Paris.

Comme des Garçons designs a one-off collection for H&M.

Vivienne Westwood showcases her ready-to-wear line, Red Label, in her first London show in twenty-five years.

2009

Renowned fashion photographer Irving Penn dies.

Tom Ford makes his debut as a film director with the film *A Single Man*.

Christopher Kane launches a new clothing line for Topshop.

Phoebe Philo is appointed chief designer for Céline.

The American first lady, Michelle Obama, wears a Junya Watanabe cardigan during a visit to London. (**31**)

London-based designer Erdem gains international popularity after both Sarah Brown, the wife of the then British prime minister, and Samantha Cameron, the wife of the UK's Conservative Party leader, appear in his designs.

2010

Alexander McQueen commits suicide. (**32**)

Marios Schwab is appointed head designer for Halston.

Kenzo celebrates its fortieth anniversary.

Picture details are on page 254.

Contemporary Fashion

Rebecca Arnold, *Fashion: A Very Short Introduction*, Oxford (Oxford University Press) 2009

Rebecca Arnold, *Fashion, Desire and Anxiety: Image and Morality in the Twentieth Century*, London (I.B. Tauris) 2001

Andrew Bolton, *The Supermodern Wardrobe*, London (V&A Publishing) 2002

Susan Bordo, *Unbearable Weight: Feminism, Western Culture and the Body*, Los Angeles (University of California) 1995

Sarah E. Braddock and Marie O'Mahoney, *Techno Textiles*, London (Thames & Hudson) 1998

Christopher Breward, *The Culture of Fashion*, Manchester (Manchester University Press) 1995

Christopher Breward, *Fashion*, Oxford (Oxford University Press) 2003

Christopher Breward and David Gilbert (eds), *Fashion's World Cities*, Oxford (Berg) 2006

Stella Bruzzi and Pamela Church Gibson (eds), *Fashion Cultures: Theories, Explanations and Analysis*, London (Routledge) 2001

Anne Brydon and Sandra Niessen, *Consuming Fashion: Adorning the Transnational Body*, Oxford (Berg) 1998

Dora Chan (ed.), *Young Asian Fashion Designers*, Cologne (Daab) 2008

Elyssa da Cruz and Sandy Black, *Fashioning Fabrics: Contemporary Textiles in Fashion*, London (Black Dog Publishing) 2006

The Cutting Edge: Fashion from Japan, exhib. cat., ed. Louise Mitchell, Sydney, Powerhouse Museum, 2005

Liza Dalby, *Kimono: Fashioning Culture*, London (Vintage) 2001

Hwyel Davies, *100 New Fashion Designers*, London (Laurence King Publishing) 2008

Hwyel Davies, *Modern Menswear*, London (Laurence King Publishing) 2008

Fred Davis, *Fashion, Culture, and Identity*, Chicago (University of Chicago Press) 1992

Laura Eceiza, *Atlas of Fashion Designers*, Beverly, Mass. (Rockport Publishers) 2008

Bonnie English, *A Cultural History of Fashion in the Twentieth Century: From Catwalk to Sidewalk*, Oxford (Berg) 2007

Caroline Evans, *Fashion at the Edge: Spectacle, Modernity and Deathliness*, New Haven, Conn., and London (Yale University Press) 2007

Extreme Beauty: The Body Transformed, exhib. cat., ed. H. Koda, New York, Metropolitan Museum of Art, New Haven, Conn., and London (Yale University Press) 2004

Susannah Frankel, *Visionaries: Interviews with Fashion Designers*, London (V&A Publishing) 2001

Akiko Fukai (ed.), *Fashion: A History from the 18th to the 20th Century: The Collection of the Kyoto Costume Institute*, Cologne and London (Taschen) 2002

Brooke Hodge and Lisa Mark, *Skin and Bones: Parallel Practices in Fashion and Architecture*, London (Thames & Hudson) 2006

Terry Jones and Avril Mair (eds), *Fashion Now: i-D Selects the World's 150 Most Important Designers*, Cologne and London (Taschen) 2003

Terry Jones and Avril Mair (eds), *Fashion Now: i-D Selects the World's 150 Most Important Designers*, vol. 2, Cologne and London (Taschen) 2005

Yuniya Kawamura, *The Japanese Revolution in Paris Fashion*, Oxford (Berg) 2004

Dorinne K. Kondo, *About Face: Performing Race in Fashion and Theater*, New York and London (Routledge) 1997

Leonard Koren, *New Fashion Japan*, Tokyo (Kodansha) 1984

Suzanne Lee, *Fashioning the Future: Tomorrow's Wardrobe*, London (Thames & Hudson) 2007

Richard Martin (ed.), *The Fashion Book*, London (Phaidon Press) 2001

Valerie Mendes, *Black in Fashion*, London (V&A Publishing) 1999

Valerie Mendes and Amy De La Haye, *Twentieth-Century Fashion*, London (Thames & Hudson) 1999

Valerie Mendes and Claire Wilcox (eds), *Twentieth-Century Fashion in Detail*, London (V&A Publishing) 2009

Laura Miller, *Beauty Up: Exploring Contemporary Japanese Body Aesthetics*, Berkeley, Calif. (University of California Press) 2006

Bradley Quinn, *Techno Fashion*, Oxford (Berg) 2002

Bradley Quinn, *Textile Designers at the Cutting Edge*, London (Laurence King Publishing) 2009

Radical Fashion, exhib. cat., ed. Claire Wilcox, London, Victoria and Albert Museum, 2001

Macarena San Martin, *Future Fashion: Innovative Materials and Technology*, Barcelona (Promotora de Prensa Internacional) 2010

Scott Schuman, *The Sartorialist*, London (Penguin) 2009

Sabine Seymour, *Fashionable Technology: The Intersection of Design, Fashion, Science and Technology*, Vienna (Springer Vienna) 2008

Toby Slade, *Japanese Fashion: A Cultural History*, Oxford (Berg) 2009

Spectres: When Fashion Turns Back, exhib. cat. by Judith Clark, Antwerp, Mode Museum, and London, Victoria and Albert Museum, 2004

Valerie Steele, *Fifty Years of Fashion: From New Look to Now*, New Haven, Conn., and London (Yale University Press) 1997

Valerie Steele and Jennifer Park, *Gothic: Dark Glamour*, New Haven, Conn., and London (Yale University Press) 2008

Barbara Vinken, *Fashion – Zeitgeist: Trends and Cycles in the Fashion System*, Oxford (Berg) 2005

Simone Werle, *50 Fashion Designers You Should Know*, Munich and London (Prestel) 2010

Elizabeth Wilson, *Adorned in Dreams: Fashion and Modernity*, London (Virago) 1985

FURTHER READING

Fashion Journals
Costume: The Journal of the Costume Society, London, Costume Society
Dress: The Journal of the Costume Society of America, New York, Costume Society of America
Fashion Theory: The Journal of Dress, Body and Culture, Oxford (Berg)
Textiles, Manchester, Textile Institute
Vestoj: Journal of Sartorial Matters

Japanese Culture
Sandra Buckley (ed.), *Encyclopedia of Contemporary Japanese Culture*, London (Routledge) 2002
Gian Carlo Calza, *Japan Style*, London (Phaidon Press) 2007
Jonathan Clements and Helen McCarthy, *The Anime Encyclopedia: A Guide to Japanese Animation Since 1917*, Berkeley, Calif. (Stone Bridge Press) 2001
Roger Davies and Osamu Ikeno (eds), *The Japanese Mind: Understanding Contemporary Japanese Culture*, Boston (Tuttle Publishing) 2002
Kenya Hara, *White*, trans. Jooyeon Rhee, Baden, Switzerland (Lars Müller Publishers) 2010
Koichi Iwabuchi, *Recentering Globalization: Popular Culture and Japanese Transnationalism*, Durham, NC (Duke University Press) 2002
Sarah Lonsdale, *Japanese Style*, London (Carlton Books) 2001
Ian Luna (ed.), *Tokyolife: Art and Design*, New York (Rizzoli) 2007
Helen McCarthy, *500 Essential Anime Movies: The Ultimate Guide*, Lewes (Ilex) 2008
Helen McCarthy, *The Art of Osamu Tezuka: God of Manga*, Lewes (Ilex) 2009
Edward Saïd, *Orientalism*, reprint with a new Afterword, Harmondsworth (Penguin) 1995
Yoshio Sugimoto (ed.), *The Cambridge Companion to Modern Japanese Culture*, Cambridge and New York (Cambridge University Press) 2009
Juni'chirō Tanizaki, *In Praise of Shadows* [1933], trans. Thomas J. Harper and Edward G. Seidensticker, Rutland, Vt. (Tuttle Publishing) 1977 and London (Vintage) 2001
Paul Varley, *Japanese Culture*, 4th edn, Honolulu (University of Hawaii Press) 2000

Issey Miyake
A-POC Making: Issey Miyake and Dai Fujiwara, exhib. cat., ed. Mateo Kries and Alexander von Vegesack, Berlin, Vitra Design Museum, 2001
Laurence Benaïm, *Issey Miyake*, London (Thames & Hudson) 1997
Mark Holborn, *Issey Miyake,* Cologne (Taschen) 1995
Issey Miyake, *Bodyworks*, Tokyo (Shogakukan) 1983
Issey Miyake Making Things, exhib. cat. by Kazuko Sato and Raymond Meier, ed. Hervé Chandès, Paris, Fondation Cartier pour l'art contemporain, 1998–99
Issey Miyake Pleats Please, exhib. cat., Tokyo, Tokyo Museum of Contemporary Art, 1990
Irving Penn, *Issey Miyake: Photographs by Irving Penn*, Boston and London (Little, Brown) 1988

Rei Kawakubo
France Grand, *Comme des Garçons*, London (Thames & Hudson) 1998
Refusing Fashion: Rei Kawakubo, exhib. cat., ed. Linda Dresner, Susanne Hilberry and Marsha Miro, Detroit, Museum of Contemporary Art, 2008
Sanae Shimizu (ed.), *Unlimited: Comme des Garçons*, Tokyo (Heibonsha) 2005
Deyan Sudjic, *Rei Kawakubo and Comme des Garçons*, New York (Rizzoli) 1990
Visionaire 20: Comme des Garçons, ed. Rei Kawakubo, New York (Visionaire) 1997

Yohji Yamamoto
Francis Baudot, *Yohji Yamamoto*, London (Thames & Hudson) 1997
A Magazine Curated by Yohji Yamamoto, Antwerp, *A Magazine*, no. 2 (2005)
Yohji Yamamoto, *Talking to Myself*, Milan (Carla Sozzani) 2002
Yohji Yamamoto: An Exhibition Triptych, exhib. cat. by Frédéric Bonnet, Florence, Paris and Antwerp, 2006

Jun Takahashi
A Magazine Curated by Jun Takahashi, Antwerp, *A Magazine*, no. 4 (2006)
Madsaki and Jun Takahashi, *Gas Book*, vol. 19, Tokyo (Gas as Interface) 2005

Young Designers and Japanese Street Fashion
Shoichi Aoki, *Fruits*, London (Phaidon Press) 2001
Shoichi Aoki, *Fresh Fruits*, London (Phaidon Press) 2005
Tiffany Godoy, *Style Deficit Disorder: Harajuku Street Fashion Tokyo*, San Francisco (Chronicle Books) 2007
Tiffany Godoy and Ivan Vartanian (eds), *Japanese Goth: Art and Design*, New York (Universe Publishing) 2009
Gothic and Lolita Bible, quarterly journal, Los Angeles (Tokyopop) [various volumes]
Philomena Keet and Yuri Manabe, *Tokyo Look Book: Stylish to Spectacular, Goth to Gyaru, Sidewalk to Catwalk*, Tokyo (Kodansha International) 2007
Rico Komanoya, *Gothic Lolita Punk*, New York (Collins Design) 2009
Patrick Macias and Izumi Evers, *Japanese Schoolgirl Inferno: Tokyo Teen Fashion Subculture Handbook*, San Francisco (Chronicle Books) 2007
Masayuki Yoshinaga and Katsuhiko Ishikawa, *Gothic and Lolita*, London (Phaidon Press) 2007

Photographers
Nick Knight, *Nick Knight*, New York (Collins Design) 2009
Paolo Roversi, *Paolo Roversi: Studio*, London (Steidl) 2009
Inez van Lamsweerde and Vinoodh Matadin, *Inez van Lamsweerde and Vinoodh Matadin*, Hamburg (Gruner & Jahr) 2009

PICTURE CREDITS

The illustrations in this book have been reproduced courtesy of the following:

Collection of the Kyoto Costume Institute:
Photographs by Naoya Hatakeyama: 3, 67, 69, 71, 73, 75, 77.
Photographs by Takashi Hatakeyama: 44 (Gift of Comme des Garçons Co., Ltd.), 46 (Gift of Comme des Garçons Co., Ltd.), 47 (Gift of Comme des Garçons Co., Ltd.), 78, 79, 89, 107 (Gift of Mr. Kosuke Tsumura), 125 (Gift of Miyake Design Studio), 164, 165, 172, 182, 186, 196 (Gift of Yohji Yamamoto Inc.), 206, 208.
Photographs by Masayuki Hayashi: 111, 120, 174–75 (background image), 202, 216, 218, 220, 222, 228–29 (background image).
Photographs by Taishi Hirokawa: 50 (Gift of Mr Hiroshi Tanaka), 51 (Gift of Ms Sumiyo Koyama and Mr Hiroshi Tanaka), 66 (Gift of Comme des Garçons Co., Ltd.), 68 (Gift of Comme des Garçons Co., Ltd.), 70 (Gift of Comme des Garçons Co., Ltd.), 72 (Gift of Comme des Garçons Co., Ltd.), 74 (Gift of Comme des Garçons Co., Ltd.), 76 (Gift of Comme des Garçons Co., Ltd.), 99 (Gift of Mintdesigns Inc.), 117, 118, 121, 126, 211, 226, 230.
Photographs by Yuko Hirose: 192, 193.
Photographs by Yasushi Ichikawa: 110 (Gift of Ms Sumiyo Koyama), 124 (Gift of Miyake Design Studio).
Photograph by Kazuo Fukunaga: 90.

© Lele Acquarone/Vogue Italia, page layout Tatiana Sagona: 61, 139; page layout Laura Marino: 227. akg-images/Erich Lessing: 38. © Anrealage, photograph Mihoko Fujiawara, art direction No Design: 244. © Anzaï: 20 bottom. © Art & commerce, photograph Richard Burbridge: 91, 178, 248 (11). Courtesy Assouline Publishing, illustration Gladys Perint Palmer (*Fashion People*, 2003): 65. © François Berthoud: 171. Courtesy Hussein Chalayan: 251 (23). © Cinema Photo/Corbis: 248 (4). © Comme des Garçons Co., Ltd: 54, 59, 60, 88, 100, 119 left and right, 138, 174–77, 203, 249 (6), 250 (26). © Condé Nast Archive/Corbis: 37, 248 (2), 248 (9). © Eley Kishimoto: 249 (16). © Final Home, Kosuke Tsumura 106, 107. © Firstview: 32 top left, 56, 205, 209, 213, 228–29 insets, 231 left and right, 232, 233, 251 (29). © Timothy Greenfield-Sanders: 17 bottom, 250 (20). Courtesy Hanae Mori Haute Couture: 28 bottom, 248 (3). © Ben Hassett: 141. © Taro Horiuchi, photograph YuichiIhara: 239. © Kenzo, Hans Feurer/Wib: 248 (1). © Nick Knight: 19, 31 top, 163, 166–69. © Kirby Koh with special thanks to Comme des Garçons Co., Ltd: 101. © Annie Leibovitz: 94–95, 190–91. © Peter Lindbergh: 36, 43, 45, 184–85. © Niall McInerney: 28 top, 31 bottom, left and right, 32 top right, 92, 97, 113, 173, 249 (8), 250 (18, 19). © Jane McLeish Kelsey: 102–103. © Yuri Manabe (photographs), Philomena Keet (captions): excerpt from *The Tokyo Look Book* (2007, reproduced with kind permission of Kodansha International): 131–36. Courtesy Matohu: 57, 250 (27). Courtesy Matthew Marks Gallery, New York, photographs Inez van Lamsweerde and Vinoodh Matadin: 20 top, 183. © Dominik Mentzos: 17 top, 249 (13). © minä perhonen, photograph R. Benegas: 241. © mintdesigns Inc., photograph Yoshitsugu Enomoto: 98, 243, 251 (24). Courtesy Miyake Design Studio, photograph Fujitsuka Mitsumasa: 80 top; photograph Yasuaki Yoshinaga: 80 bottom, 81; animation Pascal Roulin: 82–83, 251 (21); photograph Hiroshi Iwasaki/Stash: 147–59. © Sarah Moon, courtesy Michael Hoppen Gallery: 87, 187, 189, 199. Courtesy Museum of London: 29. © Akira Naka, photograph www.fashionsnap.com: 238. © Né-net, photograph Josui: 246–47. © Mika Ninagawa, courtesy of *Vogue* Nippon and the Executors of the Isabella Blow Estate: 104, 251 (30). © Ohya Design Zoo Co. Ltd: 105, 249 (15). © James Pearson-Howes: 250 (28). © Press Association: 249 (7), 251 (31). © Quadrillion/Corbis: 249 (5). © Paolo Roversi: 194, 195, 207. © Sacai, photograph Shoji Uchida: 240 (all), 251 (22). © Mikio Sakabe Co., Ltd.: 237, 242. © Derrick Santini: 251 (32). © Ellis Scott: 250 (25). Courtesy Cindy Sherman and Metro Imaging: front cover, 23, 24. © Anthea Simms: 32 bottom, 93, 109, 204, 212, 250 (17). © Somarta: 245. © Peter Stigter: 249 (14). © Hiroshi Sugimoto: 48, 53. © Tezuka Productions: 122. © Rúna Thorkelsdottir: 228–29 background. © Undercover: 127, 137, 217, 219, 221, 223, 248 (12); courtesy Undercover, photographs Dan Lecca: 58, 128. Courtesy Yohji Yamamoto, photograph Monica Feudi: 197. © Wonderbra: 248 (10). © Julien d'Ys: 55.

The publishers have made every effort to trace and contact copyright holders of the illustrations reproduced in this book; they will be happy to correct in any subsequent editions any errors or omissions that are brought to their attention.

CHRONOLOGY CAPTIONS

Pages 248–51: (**1**) Kenzo Autumn/Winter 1975–76. (**2**) Vivienne Westwood in punk attire, 1977. (**3**) See p. 28. (**4**) Richard Gere in publicity shot for *American Gigolo*, 1980. (**5**) Princess Diana in her wedding dress designed by Elizabeth and David Emanuel, 1981. (**6**) Rei Kawakubo/Comme des Garcons Autumn/Winter 1983–84. (**7**) Katharine Hamnett meeting Margaret Thatcher, 1983. (**8**) John Galliano's degree show at Central Saint Martins College of Art and Design, London, 1984. (**9**) See p. 37. (**10**) Wonderbra advertisement, 1994. (**11**) See p. 91. (**12**) See p. 217. (**13**) See pp. 16, 17. (**14**) Viktor & Rolf 'Black Hole' collection, Autumn/Winter 2001–02. (**15**) Hiroaki Ohya/Ohya Spring/Summer 2004, 'Astroboy' white synthetic jersey dress. (**16**) Detail of Eley Kishimoto 'Flash' print, 2000–present. (**17**) See pp. 32, 33. (**18**) Hussein Chalayan's degree show at Central Saint Martins College of Art and Design, London, 1993. (**19**) John Galliano for Givenchy, Spring/Summer 1996. (**20**) Rei Kawakubo costumes for *Scenario*, Merce Cunningham Dance Company, 1997; see page 16. (**21**) See pp. 80, 82–83. (**22**) See p. 240. (**23**) Hussein Chalayan Autumn/Winter 2000–01. (**24**) mintdesigns Spring/Summer 2007. (**25**) Gareth Pugh collection. (**26**) See p. 119. (**27**) See p. 57. (**28**) Carri Mundane. (**29**) Giles Deacon at his Spring/Summer 2007 catwalk presentation, wearing a Henry Holland T-shirt. (**30**) See p. 104. (**31**) Michelle Obama in Junya Watanabe cardigan, 2009. (**32**) Alexander McQueen.

ACKNOWLEDGEMENTS

Barbican Art Gallery and the Kyoto Costume Institute would like to thank the following institutions for their loans to the exhibition:

Anrealage Co., Ltd; mintdesigns Inc.; Miyake Design Studio; Yohji Yamamoto Inc.

We are grateful to each of the following for their invaluable assistance with the book and the exhibition:

Lele Acquarone; Art & Commerce; François Berthoud; Rúna Thorkelsdottir; Boekie Woekie; Richard Burbridge; Maya Shiboh and Chigako Takeda, Comme des Garçons Press; Shelley Halpern-Smith, Condé Nast London; Arthur Elgort and Sally Taylor, Arthur Elgort studio; Lyndsay Black, Firstview; Timothy Greenfield-Sanders and Mico Livingston-Beale, Timothy Greenfield-Sanders studio; Ben Hassett; Naoya Hatakeyama; Yuko Hirose; Piera Beradi, Issey Miyake Inc, London; Cristina Palumbo, Italian *Vogue*; Nick and Charlotte Knight; Cathy Layne, Kodansha Publishers; Kirby Koh; Hirofumi Kurino; Inez van Lamsweerde and Vinoodh Matadin studio; Annie Leibovitz and Jesse Blatt, Annie Leibovitz studio; Peter Lindbergh; Helen McCarthy; Niall McInerney; Jane McLeish Kelsey; Yuri Manabe; Dominik Mentzos; Trevor Carlson and Kevin Taylor, Merce Cunningham Dance Company; Jim Edwards and Charlotte Nation, Michael Hoppen Gallery; Masako Omori, The Miyake Issey Foundation; Sarah Moon; Mika Ninagawa; Gladys Perint Palmer; Bianca Wint, Proportion London; Bruno Rinaldi; Kelly Owens, Rootstein; Paolo Roversi; Cindy Sherman; Naoko Shimazu; Anthea Simms; Hiroshi Sugimoto and Eiko Tamaki, Hiroshi Sugimoto studio; Yoshimi Suzuki, Tezuka Productions; Chieri Hazu, Undercover; Riho Cyoja and Coralie Gaulthier, Yohji Yamamoto Inc.; Julien d'Ys and Marine Le Joncour, Julien d'Ys studio.

CONTRIBUTORS

Susannah Frankel
Susannah Frankel is Fashion Editor of *The Independent* and Fashion Features Director of *AnOther Magazine*. She is the author of *Visionaries: Interviews with Fashion Designers* (2001) and co-wrote the book that accompanied the exhibition *The House of Viktor & Rolf* at Barbican Art Gallery in 2008, published by Merrell.

Akiko Fukai
Akiko Fukai is Director and Chief Curator at the Kyoto Costume Institute. She has organized several major fashion exhibitions in Japan, Paris, and New York, including *Revolution in Fashion*, *Fashion in Colors* and *Luxury in Fashion Reconsidered*, and curated the exhibition *Future Beauty: 30 Years of Japanese Fashion* at Barbican Art Gallery in 2010. She is the author and editor of many books, including *Japonism in Fashion* (1994), *Fashion: A History from the 18th to the 20th Century* (2002), and *Reading Fashion from Pictures* (2009).

Philomena Keet
Philomena Keet is an anthropologist whose PhD fieldwork was carried out in the Tokyo youth fashion scene, and the author of *Tokyo Look Book* (2007). She is currently based in Tokyo, where she teaches Japanese society studies at Hosei University and is researching Japanese denim.

Hirofumi Kurino
Hirofumi Kurino was born in New York City but has spent most of his life in Tokyo. He worked in the fashion retail business for more than thirty years, during which time he co-founded the Japanese label and shop chain United Arrows. He was made an Honorary Fellow of London's Royal College of Art in 2004.

Helen McCarthy
Helen McCarthy is the author of numerous manga-themed books, including *Manga Cross-Stitch* and *The Art of Osamu Tezuka: God of Manga* (both 2009). She regularly curates the Barbican's Japanimation film programme.

Cher Potter
Cher Potter is a London-based expert in fashion futures, and runs the Creative Think Tank at the fashion-industry research, analysis and forecasting agency WGSN. She is a visiting lecturer in 'Fashion and the City' at the Architectural Association in London, and has written for various publications, including *Concept Store* and *Mirage* magazine.

Barbara Vinken
Barbara Vinken is Professor of French and Comparative Literature at Ludwig Maximilian University, Munich, and has previously held professorships at the universities of Hamburg and Zurich. She has taught as a visiting scholar at the École des hautes études en sciences sociales, Paris, New York University, Humboldt University, Berlin, and Johns Hopkins University, Baltimore. She is the author of *Fashion – Zeitgeist: Trends and Cycles in the Fashion System* (2005), among other titles.

INDEX